SPORTING EVENTS AND EVENT TOURISM: IMPACTS, PLANS AND OPPORTUNITIES

Editor:

Martin Robertson

LSA

LSA Publication No. 91

Sporting Events and Event Tourism:
Impacts, Plans and Opportunities

First published in 2006 by
Leisure Studies Association
The Chelsea School
University of Brighton
Eastbourne BN20 7SP (UK)

A catalogue record for this book
is available from the British Library.

ISBN:
1 905369 02 6
978 1 905369 02 7

Cover design, layout and typesetting by Myrene L. McFee

Cover images provided by Dreamstime.com
Photographer credits where known: Dragon boat rowers, Nicholas Rjabow;
Rock concert, Kutt Niinepuu; Baloon festival, Steven Brandt

Printed and bound by CPI Antony Rowe, Eastbourne

Contents

SPORTING EVENTS AND EVENT TOURISM: IMPACTS, PLANS AND OPPORTUNITIES: AN INTRODUCTION

Martin Robertson

Centre for Festival and Event Management, School of Marketing and Tourism, Napier University, Edinburgh (UK)

Introduction

Both the collection of papers presented here and the title given to this Leisure Studies Association (LSA) volume have grown out of the July 2005 Leisure Studies Conference entitled 'Festivals and Events: Beyond Economic Impacts'. The conference provided an arena for participants to share and discuss current developing research, thought and case examples as related to festivals and events. The papers included here provide an excellent example of how the subject area has included and grown far beyond the initial realms of description, management process or economic evaluation from which the subject area emerged. Sport Special, Mega or Hallmark events bring with them a diffuse array of questions that need investigating, developing and answering. The conference, hosted by the Centre for Festival and Event Management, Napier University, served to address some of the areas that each question covers, and the papers herein indicate both the multidisciplinary nature of responses and the increasing synergy of sciences that these hold.

The education, research and training environment for sport events and event tourism

In 1998 Heather Gibson stated that sports and tourism "suffers from a lack of integration in the realm of policy, research, and education"

(p. 45), later confirming that sport tourism has the capacity to narrate 'a wider analysis of sport as a social institution rather the micro-view of individual sports' (Gibson, 2002: p. 115). Accordingly, from this premise, the added dimension of reviewing sport and tourism in the context of special or mega sport events allows further avenues for procedural and scholarly engagement. It is both dynamic and potentially allusive.

The evolving nature of both the research environment for events and the sector itself is highlighted by Trevor Mules (2004: p. 95), who suggests that "event management is an emerging field of research and education, paralleling the growth in events themselves as part of the tourism industry". He goes on to appraise what it is about events that makes models of basic management skills (education or training) ill-defined for managing events. The uniqueness of events, the need to stage them as performances, the ever present levels of risk (financial, physical and legal), and the need to innovate gives the business environment a special and evolving dynamic. It is concluded that this requires a designated form of management training, thus opening itself to new and innovative research and pedagogic formulae. In Australia there has been a country-wide attempt to form a research agenda for event tourism (Getz, 2002), in acknowledgement of the need for establishing academic recognition in this area. Silvers, Bowdin, O'Toole and Beard Nelson (2006) opine that event management is an international industry awakening an international level of interest. Moreover, like Mules (2004), they traject that the uniqueness of events requires improvements in knowledge transfer, judging that educators, regulators, associations and practitioners look toward a clear enhancement of academic research, development and an improvement of related educational curriculum and — ultimately — the establishment of professional legitimacy.

Getz (2002: p. 13) voices the feeling of most who facilitate the development of event studies, in whichever discipline they may work: that it must not avoid challenging "the difficult theoretical, methodological and ethical issues" which it embraces. Similarly a great many would agree with Getz's assertion that the trend to house event studies in dedicated area associations (departments, schools or faculties) such as sports, tourism, hospitality or arts is more a reaction to increasing student numbers and the desire to make courses manageable (and malleable?) than it i a recognition of its own academic status. It is an interdisciplinary field, harbouring a plethora of perspectives. Getz (2002:

p. 20) summarises these perspectives under the following subheadings: *environmental; cultural and community; economic; production and programming; legal; management; psychological and political*, concluding that they should be based on the foundations of management and the study of events in society.

As Silvers *et al.* (2006: p. 195) conclude, "the establishment of events as a profession or discipline is still generating discussion and has still not been decided". Given the number of event management or event studies courses already established in the UK, North America, New Zealand and Australia (Getz, 2002; Silvers *et al.*, 2006), and rapid development of event management in Asia (Arcodia and Reid, 2003), it is a discussion with worldwide application.

By way of introduction to the chapters in this volume, the following paragraphs serve to illustrate the evolution of that discussion around many of the components that form sport tourism and event tourism; and key questions that arise from these. It is indicative of the subject area that this study is neither exhaustive nor entirely inclusive. The nature of this article and the expansive nature of this subject area do not allow it to be so. The work serves to highlight the symbiotic opportunities open to practitioners and academics that the subject field of special events and sport event tourism offers.

Sport tourism

Sport tourism can be seen to include all participation — whether as performer or audience, active or passive — in sports activity which involves and motivates leisure based travel away from usual domicile (Gibson, 1995; Standeven and Deknop, 1999; Ritchie and Adair, 2002). There has been a meteoric rise in the numbers of sport events set with a target of attracting tourists to the area in which the event is held (Penington-Gray and Holdnak, 2002). Gratton and Henry (2001) and Gratton and Taylor (2000) contend that in the UK sport events can be seen as having established a strong role for its tourism industry. There are still many questions to be asked, not least of which is 'why do sports tourists do what they do?' (Gibson, 2004). Similarly, what does or doesn't make a sport event tourist different from a sport tourist? Both of these questions have received responses (Gammon and Robinson, 2003; Kurtzman and Zauhar, 2003; Gibson, 1998, 2002, 2004) and this area of analysis continues.

Sport events and a widening policy range: the background to sport event development

Following the 2000 UK Sports Strategy, increased focus was given to sport events as tools for both economic and social benefit, with the UK Commons Select Committee on Culture, Media and Sport (third report, 2001), stating that:

> The staging of international sporting events must be seen as a means, not an end. Public support for the staging of events must be justified by proper analysis of the extent to which events are an effective means towards other ends, both sporting and non-sporting. The staging of events cannot be justified simply by vague assertions about national prestige.

Recognising that for the governing bodies the primary purpose of special events was a sporting one, but concerned that there was a need for these events to fulfil other social and economic functions, the committee recommended systematic analysis and measurement of all sport event outcomes. Further evidence of this public sector interest is shown by UKSport, the government agency accountable to the Department for Culture, Media and Sport, who commissioned Dr Adam Brown and Joanne Massey, Manchester Institute for Popular Culture, to undertake as baseline research for the sports development of the Manchester 2002 Commonwealth Games a review of literature related to impacts of major supporting events. Similarly, in 2002 the Scottish Executive pronounced that it would "deliver a viable portfolio of major events to attract visitors to Scotland, to enhance Scotland's International profile, and to maximise the economic, social and environmental benefits of events to all parts of the country" (Scottish Executive, 2002). It further proclaimed that this would encourage participation in sport at a local level and excellence in sport at a national and international level. The Scottish Executive and VisitScotland joint venture company *EventScotland* was founded as the enabling guardian of these principles in 2002.

    A 2004 literature review of the evidence base for culture, the arts and sports policy (Janet Ruiz, Scottish Executive) determined that social costs and benefits of major sporting events, with particular reference to communities, had to be evaluated. Moreover the review concluded that "there is a need for longer term research/evaluations of major events to assess whether and in what way the short-term economic benefit has been sustained" (p. 137). The same developments and conclusions can be seen in other countries. Only in respect of involvement in a mega sporting event — e.g. the Olympics — whether hosting it or bidding for it, can the linkage between social policy and sport event be seen as being applied on a global scale (Hiller, 2000). Again, this is an evolving region of analysis.

Sport events and impact evaluation

Despite the social pronouncement by governments and their agencies, evaluations of events still focus predominantly on the economic factors rather than on implicitly social or community ones. The fact remains that the economic importance of festivals and events is widely recognised by major event organisers and their funding agencies (Carlsen, 2004). More often the evaluations for these take the form of multiplier calculation derived from a balance of payment approach, i.e. an economic input and output analysis. Gratton and Taylor (2000) and Baade (1996) both state that mega sport events clearly generate additional expenditure, income and employment and are thus are appropriate to multiplier analysis — most particularly at a micro level.

Whilst the sophistication of multiplier analysis has developed considerably from a basic relationship between expenditure and employment and/or income, the fact remains that they are only estimations, albeit well-defined ones (Hughes, 1994; Crompton and McKay, 1994; Hiller, 1998). Indeed it is also the case that results vary greatly from one undertaking of multiplier analysis to another (Wall and Mathieson, 1982; Wall, 1997). Hiller (1998) comments that all evaluative analysis has tended to take a cause-effect approach, in which a predominance of study on 'mega event', such as European or World Championships or indeed the Olympics, has seen the event itself as being the main receptor and adjudicator of related benefits (as audited in the economic projections and evaluations that pre-empt and record their occurrence, respectively). Given that Olympic host cities are frequently "left to manage a legacy of negative social and economic impacts" (Higham, 1999: p. 89) one must request, as Higham suggests, that the government and other associated stakeholders undertake and attain a greater depth of response to the question, 'why and for whom do we want this event?'.

No one would choose to ignore the significance and importance of economic evaluation when attributing values to special sport events — but as an avenue of enquiry, and as an indicator of special sporting event success, it is only one of many. It is likely that many benefits have yet to be pursued as event management gains the legitimacy previously mentioned in this article.

Moving special sport events and sport event tourism out of the city

For a good length of time mega-sport events have been united with the development of cities, tending to focus — in the deliberations of academics and consultants, and in the minds and purse strings of the public sector — on their long-term enhancement potential for city tourism and the city product; and, secondly, on their role in urban regeneration (Bull, 2004). The number of articles that relate to urban development and special events pays testament to that. However there are also many opportunities for sport tourism and special events in the rural environment (MacArthur, 2003; Costa and Chalip, 2005), bringing with them opportunities for new dimensions for both the community and new forms of tourism. This remains an area for multi-disciplinary endeavour.

Loyalty and sport event tourism

Despite a well established anthology of research looking at the factors of repeat visitation to destinations *per se* there is relatively little research addressing repeat visitor segmentation and special sport events (Gandhi-Arora and Shaw, 2002: p. 46). In evaluating the motive for attending sport events, Gandhi-Arora and Shaw find that *novelty seeking* was less of a motivation characteristic than has been suggested in other tourist experience studies, and could thus be seen as less susceptible to consumer service switching (Oliver, 1999). An implication of this is that sport tourism has the capacity to create loyalty on the basis of consumer intention to visit specific events, and to benefit from consumer desire for novelty through attraction to other events. Whilst there is an ongoing discussion surrounding the related issues of consumer intention to attend events, plus their latent and inducted attitude and correlation of this to satisfaction levels (Hede, Deery and Jago, 2002), the issue of sport event visitor loyalty requires continuing multi-disciplinary investigation.

Reference to the areas of event perspective as drawn by Getz (2002) would obviously be a suitable vantage point from which to map routes of exploration.

Special sport events and the destination

In respect of the relationship between sports and their locale (destination), Higham (2005: pp. 2–4) in his analysis of prevailing literature in the field identifies ten core areas which are valuable to destination managers. These are: tourist demand; tourism development; service sector development; event sport tourism; visitor experience at tourist destination; destination profile; destination media markets; destination image; uniqueness of tourism destination, and tourism seasonality. Whilst each area has a well-developed body of data there is much to do and the progression of a better-defined multidisciplinary body of knowledge for event studies and management (as above) will aid in this.

The Chapters

Chapter 1: In employing lessons learnt from the international arena, and utilising world examples to animate points made, John Horne argues that those responsible for development of sport mega-events often choose to manage or interpret special mega-events development in a way that wilfully (or as an act of institutional collusion, or 'social amnesia') recreates the same mega-event impact failings (most notably financial loss and social displacement) or fails to take the positives further. Investigating the 'known' and 'unknowns' of involvement with sport mega-events, the article starts with an exploration of the spectacular rise of interest in mega-events by host nations and the incumbent motivations of attaining global audience, of receiving corporate sponsorship and in the selling of the host place. It then looks at the legacies to which mega-events pertain but so rarely take successfully or fully beyond the conceptual intention first voiced. It is suggested that academics and researchers have a duty to be imaginative, to respond to the 'unknown unknowns', and offer rejoinders to questions relating to all elements that comprise a sport mega-event. Concomitantly, in the final analysis, evidence of 'social amnesia' is shown within the political, economic and ideological context of a number of significant sport mega-events.

Chapter 2: Examining the Cricket World Cup 2007 in the Caribbean, Leslie-Ann Jordan records and forms a critique of the official managerial process and the required orchestration of an event to be held in eight countries with separate and independent governments. In attempting to address the potential economic, social-cultural and political impacts of this mega-event, the stakeholders, she suggests, have set themselves a Herculean task. In drawing analysis from public government, agency and media sources, Jordan provides a rich study of the challenges of managing a truly unique mega-event, extrapolating from this a range of critical success factors. The paper as a whole should, as she suggests, be seen as a launching pad for future research in mega-event management *per se*, with particular ramifications for the management of mega-events held in small island developing states.

Chapter 3: Debbie Sadd and Caroline Jackson provide an extensive investigation of the potential role of the 2012 Summer Olympic and Paralympics for regeneration of Weymouth and the neighbouring Isle of Portland. First mapping and updating the theoretical boundaries identified as reasons for hosting Mega-Events, the authors then test resort lifecycle theories as a guidance model within the context of using events as resort regeneration. In positioning their investigation of the event within the tourism planning procedures for Weymouth and Portland, Sadd and Jackson detect the strategic shortfalls and strategic opportunities that the event offers for area regeneration. Having evaluated the possible and appropriate impacts of tourism in 2012, the paper then draws up a strategic action framework for Weymouth and Portland. Significantly, the research for this paper was undertaken prior to the announcement that London had won the bid to host the Olympics. It is possible the findings are all the richer for this reason.

Chapter 4: Phil Binks and Bob Snape also invite reference to the immediacy of the research and writing up of their paper with the announcement on the first day of the LSA 2005 conference that London was to host the 2012 Olympic Games. Here they request that the excitement of the announcement should have also caused an awakening to and addressing of the issues surrounding the often unholy alliance of the public, private and voluntary agencies that sport mega or special event partnerships form. In analysing the development of the Bolton Arena, a large sports venue, they direct analysis to many of the issues that these partnerships must face in ensuring that the post-event actions meet the pre-event plans. The research was exercised through examination of documentary sources and semi-structured interviews with the arena's governing body and local government officers. The authors conclude that a number of issues, both political and physical (most notably the proximity to the Manchester Commonwealth Games, and the apparent funding opportunities that this spurred), served to distort the continuity of the policies and plans for the stadium.

Chapter 5: From an initial recording of the growth and definition of sports tourism and special event tourism in Canada, Margaret E. Johnstone and G. David Twynam focus on the motivation and behaviour of spectators at special sporting events: an event form they appraise as bridging both sport tourism and special event tourism. Research was undertaken in Thunder Bay, Ontario, Canada, principal town for the Nordic World Ski Championship. Their research sought to assess spectator involvement at a number of levels. The results of two questionnaires, one for resident spectators and one for non-resident spectators of the event, indicated that non-residents were significantly more involved in the event than the residents, although both groups showed high levels of recreational and competitive behaviour. The authors go on to suggest further process to add depth to the understanding of spectator behaviour.

Chapter 6: As the first phase in a longitudinal study of the legacy of the 2005 Women's European Championship, in the North West of England, Barbara Bell presents and interprets the initial findings in respect of their part in the longer term potential of the legacy. She also examines the issues surrounding analysis of the impacts of the event, most particularly in assessing participation in women's football in the region as a result of the Championship. Her evaluation draws on a context-mechanism-outcome matrix methodology, comparing and appraising mapped-out legacy expectations with outcomes of legacy programme activities. Her work, she explains, is part of a further exploration of opportunities for sport access and perception by women to sport, and the function and meaning it can be seen to attribute to different groupings.

Chapter 7: Leanne White's work assesses the opening and closing ceremonies of a mega-event of world renown, the Sydney 2000 Olympic Games. Concerned with determining the symbols and images utilised to transmit 'Australia' and 'Australianness' in these ceremonies, a mixture of qualitative semiotic analysis and quantitative content analysis methodologies were employed for this phenomenological study. Investigation of the ceremony components and 'formalities' allows a deconstruction of the broadcasted images of Australia. The conclusions both commend (the event was a success, and the images conveyed appropriate and well-received) and criticise ('cultural cringe', as White calls it, could have happened) how the games ceremony conveyed a national identity.

Conclusions

Bringing these papers together opens a dialogue that spans four continents (and by association touches on all seven). The area of sports tourism special and mega event study and analysis is one which brings with it a great many pedagogical, philosophical and managerial disciplines. The body of knowledge that is growing around sports tourism and event tourism indicates at least a partial rescission of the sense of academic illegitimacy that Gibson (1998: p68) suggests sport and tourism has suffered for many years at the hands of the 'parent disciplines'. The articles contained in this publication add legitimacy, giving not only sport and tourism more strength in its multi-disciplinary research base, but also contributing to the development of sport event and special sport event tourism as a research area.

Sport mega-events will continue to inspire hyper-interest and awe in many, whether they are part of the potential audience, the community, or in the realm of politics, the media, in academia, or involved in event operation, research and practice. Impacts, plans and opportunities (as demonstrated in all the articles included here) may be lost in the sense of other-ness that sport mega or special events are often seen to evoke. I would suggest that any such attitude of holiness or unchecked singularity surrounding the management, partnerships and hosting of mega-events must be replaced by a legitimate event management discipline. This will ensure that it is checked, analysed and developed appropriately. The proper development of study and research in events as a legitimate discipline would positively demand this.

References

Arcodia, C. and Reid, S. (2003) 'Goals and objectives of event management associations', *Journal of Convention and Exhibition Management* Vol. 5 No. 1: pp. 57–75.

Baade, R (1996) 'Professional sports as a catalyst for metropolitan economic development', *Journal of Urban Affairs* Vol. 18, No. 1: pp. 1-17.

Bull, C. (2004) 'Sports tourism destination resource analysis', in J. Higham (ed): pp. 25-38.

Brown, A. and Massey, J (2001) *Literature review — the impact of major sporting events, The sports development impact of the Manchester 2002 Commonwealth Games: Initial baseline research.* London: UK Sport.

Carlsen, J., Getz, D. and Soutar, G. (2001) 'Event evaluation research', *Event Management* Vol. 6: pp. 247-257.

Carlsen, J. (2004) 'The economics and evaluation of festivals and events' in Yeoman, I., Robertson, M., Ali-Knight, J., Drummond, A. and McMahon-Beattie, U. (eds) *Festival and events management: An international arts and culture perspective.* Oxford: Elsevier Butterworth-Heinemann, pp. 246-259.

Costa, C.A. and Chalip, L. (2005) 'Adventure Sport Tourism in rural revitalisation', *European Sport Management Quarterly.* Vol. 5, No. 3: pp. 257-279.

Crompton, J. and McKay, S.L. (1994) 'Measuring the economic impacts of festivals and events', *Festival Management and Event Tourism: An International Journal* 2: pp. 33-43.

Daniels, M.J., Norman, W.C. and Henry, M.S. (2004) 'Estimating income effects of a sport tourism event', *Annals of Tourism Research* Vol. 31, No: 1: pp. 180-199.

Getz, D. (2002) 'Event studies and event management: On becoming an academic discipline', *Journal of Hospitality and Tourism Management.* Vol. 9, No. 1: pp. 12-23.

Gandhi-Arora, R. and Shaw, R.W. (2002) 'Visitor loyalty in sport tourism: An empirical investigation', *Current Issues in Tourism* Vol. 5, No.1: 45-53.

Gammon, S. and Robinson, T. (2003) 'Sport and tourism: a conceptual framework' *Journal of Sport Tourism.* Vol. 8, No. 1: pp. 21-36.

Gibson, H. (1998) 'Sport tourism: A critical analysis of research', *Sport Management Review,* Vol. 1: pp. 45-76.

—— (2002) 'Sport tourism at a crossroad? Consideration for the future', in S. Gammon and J. Kurtzman (eds) *Sport tourism: Principles and practice* (LSA Publication No. 76). Eastbourne: Leisure Studies Association.

—— (2004) 'Understanding sports tourism experience', in M. Weed and C. Bull (eds) *Sports tourism: Participants, policy and providers.* Oxford: Elsevier Butterworth Heinemann: pp. 57-72.

—— (1995) 'The wide world of sports tourism', *Parks and Recreation*: p. 100.

Gratton, C. and Henry, I. (eds) (2001) *Sport in the City: The role of sport in economic and social regeneration.* London: Routledge.

Gratton, C. and Taylor, P. (2000) *Economics of Sport and Recreation.* London: Spon Press.

Gratton, C., Dobson, N. and Shilli, S. (2000) 'The economic importance of major sports events: A case-study of six events', *Managing Leisure* No. 5: pp. 17-28..

Hede, A., Deery, M. and Jago, L.K. (2002) 'A conceptual model of satisfaction with special events: A destination branding context', Paper presented at 2002 CAUTHE conference *Tourism and Hospitality on the Edge.*

Higham, J. (1999) 'Commentary — Sport as an avenue of tourism development: An analysis of the positive and negative impacts of sport tourism', *Current Trends in Tourism* Vol. 2, No. 1: pp. 82-90.

Higham, J. (ed.) (2005) *Sport Tourism Destination: Issues, opportunities and analysis* Oxford: Elsevier Butterworth Heinemann.

Hiller, H.H. (1998) 'Assessing the impact of mega-events: a linkage model', *Current Issues in Tourism* 1/1: 47-57.

—— (2000) 'Mega-events, urban boosterism and growth strategies: an analysis of the objectives and legitimations of the Cape Town 2004 Olympic bid.' *International Journal of Urban and Regional Research.* Vol. 22, No. 2: pp.439-458.

Hughes, H. (1994) 'Current Issues: Tourism Multiplier studies: a more judicious approach' *Tourism Management* Vol. 15, No. 6: pp. 403-06.

Macarther, S. (2003) 'Can small events be used as part of a destination marketing strategy to generate tourism to a non-tourist centre?', *Journal of Hospitality and Tourism Management* Vol. 10: pp. 41-50.

Mules, T. (2004) 'Case study — evolution in event management: The Gold Coast's Winter Festival', *Event Management* Vol. 9: pp 95-101.

Oliver, R. L. (1999) 'Whence consumer loyalty?', *Journal of Marketing* Volume 63 Special Issue: pp. 33-44.

Penington-Gray, L. and Holdnak, A. (2002) 'Out of the stands and into the community: Using sports events to promote a destination', *Event Management* Vol. 7: pp. 177-186.

Richie, B. and Adair, D (2002) 'Editorial: The growing recognition of sport tourism', *Current Issues in Tourism* Vol. 5, No. 1: pp. 1-6.

Scottish Executive (2002) *Scotland's major event strategy 2003-2015 — competing on an international stage.* Edinburgh: Scottish Executive: Edinburgh.

Scottish Executive Education Department/ Janet Ruiz (2004) *A literature review of the evidence base for culture, the arts, and sport policy.* Edinburgh: Scottish Executive.

Sportscotland (2001) *The economic importance of sport in Scotland in 2001,* Research Digest No. 95. Glasgow: Sportscotland.

Standeven, J. and Deknop, P. (1999) *Sport tourism.* Champaign: Human Kinetics.

ABOUT THE CONTRIBUTORS

Barbara Bell, PhD, is currently lecturer in sport and leisure management at Edge Hill in Lancashire. Previously she was Field Leader for Sports Studies at Warrington Collegiate Institute and worked in the management of community sport recreation for ten years. Her main research interests lie in youth sport, and in particular the evaluation of policy and programmes, particularly where they involve the development of personal and social capital. She is currently developing a book based on her recently completed PhD, applying critical realist evaluation approaches to youth sport and coaching. The current project on the Euro 2005 event has lead to further work on football and social marketing, and other work in women's football development, including cross cultural perspectives of the game in Britain.

Phil Binks is currently a Senior Lecturer in the Sport Leisure and Tourism Management Department at The University of Bolton. He is Programme Leader for the BA Sports Development and involved in the delivery of the MA in Community Sports Development. Phil's current research interests include sport and community safety and the use of physical activity as an agency for social inclusion.

John Horne, PhD, is Senior Lecturer in the Sociology of Sport and Leisure at the University of Edinburgh. He has published many articles and book chapters on sport, leisure and popular culture and is the author of *Sport in consumer culture* (2006, Palgrave) and co-author of *Understanding sport* (1999, Spon, with Alan Tomlinson and Garry Whannel). He is the co-editor of several collections with Wolfram Manzenreiter including *Sports mega-events* (2006, *Sociological review monograph*, Blackwell), *Football goes east: Business, culture and the people's* *game in China, Japan and Korea* (2004, Routledge) and *Japan, Korea and the 2002 World Cup* (2002, Routledge). He has also edited two Leisure Studies Association publications: *Leisure cultures, consumption and commodification* (2001) and masculinities: Leisure cultures, identities and consumption (2000, with Scott Fleming).

Caroline Jackson is Senior Lecturer in the School of Services Management, Bournemouth University. She is Programmer Leader for the BA (Hons) and MSc Events Management courses and is continuing her research interests in the area of events and the consumer experience. She has published and presented articles on teaching, learning and assessment. She was awarded a Learning and Teaching Fellowship by Bournemouth University 2005-6 on the basis of her work on live student events and the use of e-learning. She is a partner in the FDTL5 project 'Towards inclusive assessment: unleashing creativity'. She is Secretary of the Association for Events Management Education.

Margaret Johnston, H.BSc., Ph.D, has worked in the School of Outdoor Recreation, Parks and Tourism, Lakehead University since 1990. She was the Director of the School of Outdoor Recreation, Parks and Tourism for six years and now teaches first year courses in management and upper year tourism courses. Her research looks at special events, community involvement and change, and tourism in the polar regions. Contributions include examining the broad context of regulation in tourist behaviour in the Arctic and Antarctic, assessing the long-term impacts for communities of hosting special events, and examining resident views of community change economic developments. Dr. Johnston has worked with groups such as The International Ecotourism Society and the Worldwide Fund for Nature (WWF Arctic Programme) on tourism projects. Current research involves exploring community capacity building and other social legacies of hosting special events.

Leslie-Ann Jordan, Ph. D., is a Hospitality and Tourism Lecturer at the University of the West Indies, Department of Management Studies, Trinidad and Tobago, West Indies. She holds a B.Sc. in Tourism Management from the University of the West Indies and a Post-graduate Diploma and Ph.D. from the University of Otago, New Zealand. Her research interests include tourism development in small island states with special reference to the Anglophone Caribbean; tourism planning and development and tourism policy and decision-making. More recent research focuses on resort planning and development in the Caribbean and event management. She is the author of *Institutional arrangements for tourism in small twin-island states of the Caribbean* (Routledge 2004).

Martin Robertson is an undergraduate programmes leader and lecturer in the School of Marketing and Tourism, Napier University, Edinburgh. He is also a committee member of the Centre for Festival and Event Management (CFEM). He has presented papers, and authored and edited published texts in the areas of urban tourism; festival and event management; destination marketing, and the management of narrative as a leisure management function. He is a founding committee member of the Association of Event Management Educators (AEME). Current research activities include analysis of sport special events and its role in the co-branding of rural areas.

Deborah Sadd is a part-time lecturer at Bournemouth University in the School of Services Management. She teaches on the BA Events Management and BA Leisure Management Degree Programmes. Debbie completed a Tourism and Planning Management Masters degree in September 2004 with distinction. Research for Masters carried out in Weymouth and Portland, Dorset an Olympic Venue during Summer 2004, prior to the successful 2012 Olympic Bid. This research project is ongoing. She also completed in 2006 a Masters in Event Management and continues to advise local charities on fundraising issues as well as other private consultancy work in the Events Business.

Bob Snape, PhD, is a Principal Lecturer in the Department of Sport, Leisure and Tourism Management at the University of Bolton. His research interests include the political, cultural and social contexts of community sport development and cultural aspects of leisure in the period 1850-1914, particularly those relating to reading, public libraries, museums and art galleries. He is due to publish a chapter on the imperial context of the National Home Reading Union in a forthcoming book by the University of Toronto Press. He is also working on a number of community research projects on Asian communities and asylum seekers.

David Twynham, PhD, accepted the position of Dean, School of Tourism at UCC, Thompson Rivers University in 1988. His research focuses on nature based tourism opportunities and market segmentation, local views of tourism development in the north, the Arctic and the Caribbean, the development of principles and codes of conduct for tourism, and motivations and behaviours of special event spectators and volunteers. He has been extensively involved in the Arctic tourism guidelines project initiated by the World Wide Fund for Nature and has also participated in the Ecotourism Society's project in the Caribbean that explored local interest in marine ecotourism guidelines. He and his research colleague, Margaret Johnston, have studied special and major events, including longitudinal studies of spectators and volunteers. Their work has sought to understand the contributions of local community volunteers and the impacts of special events on communities. Recent publications include: Twynam, G.D., and Johnston, M.E (2004) 'Changes in host community reactions to a special sporting event', *Current Issues in Tourism* 7(3), 242-261; Twynam, G.D., Farrell, J.M. and Johnston, M.E (2003) 'Leisure and volunteer motivation at a special sporting event', *Leisure/Loisir* 27, (3-4) 363-377; Twynam, G.D., and Johnston, M.E. (2002) 'The use of sustainable tourism practices', *Annals of Tourism Research* 29 (4) 1165-1168; Payne, R.J., Twynam, G.D., and Johnston, M.E. (2001) 'Tourism, sustainability and the social milieu in Lake Superior's north shore', in McCool, S. and Moisey, N. (eds) *Tourism, recreation and sustainability: Linking culture and environment.* CABI.

Leanne White BA, DipEd, BEd, MA is a lecturer in undergraduate and postgraduate Marketing at Victoria University in Melbourne, Australia. She has taught Marketing, Public Relations, Communications, Media Studies and Australian Studies at universities since 1988. Leanne has also worked in the areas of public relations, research and policy in government and higher education. Leanne's research interests include: advertising, national identity, commercial nationalism, Australian popular culture, and the Olympic movement. Leanne's Master of Arts research thesis (1995) was entitled 'Commercial Nationalism: Images of Australia in Television Advertising'. Her doctoral thesis, which examines manifestations of official and commercial nationalism at the Sydney 2000 Olympic Games, is currently being completed.

THE 'UNKNOWN KNOWNS'
OF SPORTS MEGA-EVENTS

John D. Horne

**Physical Education, Sport and Leisure Studies,
The University of Edinburgh (UK)**

Introduction

Maurice Roche (2000: p. 1) suggests that mega-events are best under-stood as "large-scale cultural (including commercial and sporting) events, which have a dramatic character, mass popular appeal and international significance". Detailed analysis of sports mega-events, such as the FIFA association football World Cup and the Summer Olympic Games, enables consideration of several overlapping and intersecting issues of contemporary social scientific interest.[1] What defines these sports events as "mega" is that they are "discontinuous" (Roberts, 2004: p. 108), out of the ordinary, international and simply big in composition. What Roberts refers to as "megas" have the ability to transmit pro-motional messages to billions of people via television and other develop-ments in telecommunications. "Megas" have attracted an increasingly more international audience and composition. The 2004 Athens Olympic Games for example could potentially reach 3.9 billion people. 35,000 hours were dedicated to its media coverage — an increase of 27 per cent over the Summer Olympics held in Sydney in 2000 (www.ioc.com). It is these leisure industry "supernovas" (Roberts, 2004: p. 112) that this paper focuses on.

Writing in *The Guardian* Slavoj Zizek (2005) noted that when the US Defence Secretary, Donald Rumsfeld, engaged in a little amateur philo-sophy about the situation in Iraq in March 2003 he missed an important dimension. Rumsfeld stated the following: "There are known knowns. There are things we know that we know. There are known unknowns. That is to say, there are things that we know that we don't know. But there are also unknown unknowns. There are things we do not know we

1

don't know" (to listen to this and other soundbites from Donald Rumsfeld visit the BBC Radio 4 website www.bbc.co.uk/radio4/news/bh/rumsfeld.shtml). Zizek added that Rumsfeld forgot to add the crucial fourth term, "'unknown knowns', things we don't know that we know'".

Whilst Rumsfeld suggested that the main dangers in the confrontation with Iraq were the 'unknown unknowns', in this paper I am going to agree with Zizek and suggest that it may be the 'unknown knowns' that are more pernicious. This is as true for sports mega-events as for military operations. I want to suggest that it is essential to look critically at the assumptions, beliefs and obscene practices that are often suppressed or even repressed — the 'unknown knowns' of sports mega-events. I shall argue that when it comes to sports mega-events, politicians, senior administrators of sport, corporate leaders and even some academics encourage the pretence that we do not know about many of the routine practices that actually underpin them. Information will be used from studies of sports mega-events that have taken place, or are planned, in Africa, Asia, Australia, Europe and North America to illustrate the four 'knowns', but with the main focus on the 'unknown knowns'.

Known knowns (banalities)

Since 1992, when the Summer and Winter Olympic Games took place in the same year for the last time, there has been a two-year cycle of sports mega-events.[2] The Summer Olympic Games shares its year with the European Football Championships, organised by the Union of European Football Associations (UEFA), whilst the Winter Olympics shares its year with the FIFA football World Cup finals and the Commonwealth Games. Beside the banal observations that can be made about the 'what, where and when' of these events — in 1992 Barcelona and Albertville were hosts of the summer and winter Olympics, in 1994 Lillehammer hosted the Winter Olympics and the USA hosted the football World Cup finals, in 1996 Atlanta hosted the summer Olympics, and so on — it is evident that the enthusiasm to host as well as participate in sports mega-events like the Olympic Games and the FIFA World Cup has grown.[3]

The expansion and growing attraction of mega-events has been for three main reasons. First, new developments in the technologies of mass communication, especially the development of satellite television, have created unprecedented global audiences for events like the Olympics and the World Cup. This, in turn, has meant that the television revenues available to host cities have grown exponentially since the mid-1970s. Indeed, where the television rights for Montreal 1976 sold for less than US$ 30 million, only eight years later the rights for the Los Angeles Olympics brought in more than US$ 240 million, and by Sydney 2000 this had risen to over US$1 billion (Roche, 2000). Jacques Rogge, president of the International Olympic Committee (IOC), told *The Financial Times* in May 2005 that he expected total television rights for the Olympic Games to rise to US$ 3.5 billion by 2012.

Second, the influx of corporate sponsorship money into the Olympics, which began with Los Angeles in 1984, has provided another important source of income for host cities. Together, these two 'revenue streams' — and we should remember that the strategic appeal of the Olympics to corporate sponsors is directly related to the size of the television audiences — have transformed the economic calculus associated with hosting the Games. We need only recall that, in the aftermath of Montreal's huge debts, Los Angeles was the only serious bidder for the 1984 Olympics; but now, both the Olympics and the World Cup have become extended extravaganzas of promotional opportunities (Whitson, 1998). Long gone are the days, as in 1966, when FIFA could simply announce that the next four World Cup finals would be played in Mexico, Germany, Argentina and Spain (Katwala, 2000: p. 63).

Finally, a third reason why interest in hosting sports mega-events has grown, is that just as they are seen as useful in the selling of all manner of commercial products, so too are they seen as valuable promotional opportunities for cities and regions, showcasing their attractions to global audiences and helping to attract tourism and outside investment. Elsewhere Hannigan (1998) has identified the growth of "urban entertainment destinations" (UEDs) as one of the most significant developments transforming cities throughout the developed world since the 1980s. The convergence of three trends — the rationalization of the entertainment industries ("McDonaldization"), theming ("Disneyization"), and synergies between previously discrete activities such as shopping, dining out, entertainment and education (what some regard as a feature of "postmodernization") — have helped produce what Hannigan calls the "fantasy city". These trends raise questions about the social distribution of the supposed benefits of urban development initiatives, including mega-events and festivals. Who actually benefits? Who is excluded?

The production of spaces for urban play has been further assisted by developments in politics: in particular, what some have referred to as the growth of the "competition state" (Jessop 2002) and the "entrepreneurial city" (Harvey, 1989). This phenomenon has seen urban and regional governments compete with one another to offer incentives to private developers of sports and entertainment complexes, and even downtown entertainment districts, in the belief that this is the best (or only) way to bring investment, shopping, and vitality back to decaying downtowns. The problem is that developers have been able to extract public subsidies and tax holidays from governments desperate for their business, while the same governments have been cutting back, sometimes severely, on social welfare spending. Both neo-liberal, and "neo-labour", political ideas have meant different objectives for community development, and different definitions of the public good. There has been a shift away from notions of citizenship involving 'rights' to high-quality public services, towards ideals of consumerism in which the best cities are those that have 'world class' shopping. The growth of the "global sport-media-tourism complex" (Nauright, 2004: p. 1334) also leads in some respect to greater secrecy and lack of transparency on the part of the organizations involved. For Zygmunt Bauman (1998: 8) this impact on democratic processes of consultation and discussion is part of the "Great War of Independence from Space" of the last quarter of the twentieth century. There has been " a consistent and relentless wrenching of the decision-making centres, together with the calculations which ground the decisions such centres make, free from territorial constraints — the constraints of locality".

Known unknowns (uncertainties)

Given all the unpredictability and uncertainties surrounding major international sports mega-events, why do governments and cities compete for the right to host them? What are the trade-offs and opportunity costs of doing so? Do such events ultimately deliver the benefits, economic and otherwise, that their proponents proclaim? The arguments for hosting sports mega-events are usually articulated in terms of sportive as well as economic and social benefits for the hosting nation. Yet research has pointed out significant gaps between forecast and actual outcomes, between economic and non-economic rewards, between the experience of mega-events in advanced and in developing societies. To take one example, predictions of a million sports tourists to watch the FIFA World Cup in Japan and South Korea in May and June, 2002 were wildly optimistic. Japan attracted only 30,000 more visitors and South Korea reported the same number as the previous year (Horne and Manzenreiter, 2004: p. 197; see also Matheson and Baade, 2003). The "legacies" — whether social, cultural, environmental, political, econom,ic or sporting — are the 'known unknowns' of sports mega-events. They create the allure of the games — perhaps especially for developing economies (Black and van der Westhuizen, 2004). At the same time it seems evident (known) that forecasts are nearly always wrong. Since the late 1970s (and the Montreal Olympics especially) a major concern in considerations of sports mega-events has been the gap between the forecast and actual impacts on economy, society and culture.

Thus there are several comparisons to be drawn between the study of sports mega-events and the analyses of Bent Flyvbjerg and his associates into the planning of megaprojects (see for example Flyvbjerg, et al., 2003). They suggest that, with respect to the impacts of megaprojects, "Rarely is there a simple truth...What is presented as reality by one set of experts is often a social construct that can be deconstructed and reconstructed by other experts" (Flyvbjerg et al. 2003: p. 60). Promoters of multi-billion dollar megaprojects, including sports stadia and other infrastructure, have consistently, systematically and self-servingly misled governments and the public in order to get projects approved. There is another fantasy world of underestimated costs, overestimated revenues, underestimated environmental impacts and over-valued economic development effects. As Flyvbjerg et al. (2003: p. 7) suggest more often than not "power play, instead of commitment to deliberative ideals, is often what characterises megaproject development". Proper social impact assessments and full public consultation before submitting bids is required if mega-events, as megaprojects, are to regain public support and become more democratically accountable achievements (Flyvbjerg et al., 2003). Otherwise they remain based on dubious, unethical and possibly illegal practices[4].

Unknown unknowns (Insecurities)

The phrase "unknown unknowns" suggests that either we lack the information to know that we don't know something, or there are things out there that we cannot even begin to imagine. Certainly it would be possible to construct a rather lengthy list of different events, locations and associated risks, to do with security or commercial sponsorship for example, that sports mega-event could comprise and face. Academics and researchers need to be more imaginative and ready and willing to respond to these questions than politicians. One way they can do this is by reflecting on the fourth set of knowns — the 'unknown knowns', to which we shall now turn.

Unknown knowns (anxieties)

'Unknown knowns' are things we don't believe we know or remember that we know. They are the things that we repress and that can cause us anxiety. This form of social amnesia is best understood within the broader political/economic/ideological context in which debates about the distribution of the opportunity costs and benefits of hosting sports events and using sport as a form of social and economic regeneration have taken shape.

Claims and counter-claims are issued, with the emphasis of advocates typically on the *economic* impacts of hosting sports events (Roberts, 2004: pp. 116–120; UK Sport, 1999). As the UK Sport report *Measuring Success* 2 noted, major international spectator events generate "significant economic activity and media interest" (UK Sport, 2004: p. 11). But how that activity is distributed and who actually benefits are the key questions asked by sceptics. Social redistribution versus growth machine arguments about sports mega-events such as the Olympic Games revolve around the spin-offs.

In the UK and Australia hosting international sporting events have been the main stimuli for using sport for economic regeneration. In response to urban decline Glasgow, Sheffield, Manchester and Birmingham have invested heavily in the sports infrastructure so that each has a portfolio of major sports facilities capable of holding major sports events. In addition, three of them have been designated as a "National City of Sport". While the World Student Games held in Sheffield in 1991 was entered into without any serious impact study, it produced a loss of £180million, and the resulting debt has added "just over £100 to annual council tax bills and will not be repaid until 2013" (www.strategy.gov.uk/2002/sport/report). Following several failed bids to host the Olympics in the 1980s and 1990s, UK cities aimed to host lesser major sports events. The European football championship in 1996 and the Commonwealth Games staged in Manchester in 2002.

In Australia a similar strategy has been adopted at state level — states provide cities with the funds to bid for international sports events. It was estimated at the end of the 1990s that 5 per cent of Australia's tourism income of around US$16 billion was derived from major events. Australia's cities (Adelaide, Melbourne, Brisbane and Sydney) used sport as part of an economic development strategy in response to city/state rivalry — to establish a strong tourism industry. Cities in the USA placed a huge investment in the infrastructure — such as stadium developments for the big four professional team sports. Such efforts at "urban booster-ism" saw more and more cities competing to offer professional teams facilities. Teams sat back and let bidding cities "bid up the price". By the end of the 1990s there were 30 major stadium construction projects in progress — nearly one-third of the total professional sports infrastructure in the USA. The total value was estimated at US$ 9 billion.

Reviewing attempts to use sport as a means of urban regeneration in the USA, Europe and Australia Gratton and Henry (2001) concluded, "the potential benefits … have not yet been clearly demonstrated". Some places have been successful in harnessing social and urban regeneration plans to the sports mega-event. In this respect Barcelona has been acclaimed throughout Europe and the rest of the world as how to do it. But even apparent winners have created problems for themselves, including social polarisation through low cost housing soon reaching prices unaffordable for any but the most affluent for example (Hughes 1992, see also Vázquez Montalbán 1990/1992, 1991/2004).

Much North American research suggests that sports mega-events and mega projects (such as stadium construction) shift public resources to private corporations (Coakley and Donnelly, 2004; Crompton, 2001; Baade and Matheson; 2002). In a similar critique, Australian sociologist Helen Wilson has argued that as part of an increasingly global media system, sports mega-events spectacularize urban space "in the interests of global flows rather than local communities" (Wilson, 1996: p. 617). Likewise, C. Michael Hall has questioned whether the people of Sydney really did benefit from hosting the 2000 Olympics: "The irony is that government, which is meant to be serving the public interest, is instead concentrating its interests on entrepreneurial and corporate rather than broader social goals" (2001: p. 180; see also Lenskyj, 2002). Cities seek to host, but nations and citizens must back and ultimately pay for bids to host mega-events.

Cashman (2003) identifies four periods during which the impact of the summer games on Olympic host cities is debated. During the preparation of the bid and competition to win the right to host mega-events such as the Olympic Games "bidding wars" are particularly apparent (see Sugden and Tomlinson, 2002 on the bidding wars surrounding the 2006 FIFA World Cup). This is also when overestimated benefits and underestimated cost forecasts are likely to be stated with most conviction and yet often prove to be wildly inaccurate. An email circulated by British Prime Minister Tony Blair a month before the decision was made about the 2012 Summer Olympics claimed, amongst other things, that "A London victory on 6 July would mean: thousands of new jobs, a boost to tourism across the UK, the chance to host athlete preparation camps up and down the country" (tony.blair@reply-new.labour.org.uk). During the seven year preparation period from the host being announced to the actual event, in addition to the infrastructure development, attempts to "manufacture consent" to the bid have been, and will be, made by controlling mega-event related news in the media (Lenskyj, 2004, 1996). In addition legislative changes are introduced to create an 'Olympic bubble' within which sponsors can enjoy immunity from dissent as well as ambush marketing. Thus in the Queen's speech to MPs and peers at the state opening of the British Parliament in May 2005, enabling legislation was included that will now be enacted in order to protect the investments of sponsors and advertisers (*The Guardian*, 18 May 2005). Such forms of legislation help to create a climate of censorship (and in some cases self-censorship) in which journalists act as cheerleaders and critical voices are marginalised. Despite changes of personnel and rules, considerable secrecy and lack of transparency continue to pervade the undemocratic organizations that run sports 'megas' (Hoberman, 1995; Krüger, 1993). Those that challenge this, or write about it critically, may become *persona non grata* to the mega-event organisers.

During the mega-event the identities of local people are meant to conform to the (generally) positive stereotypes contained in pre-event publicity and the opening ceremonies. A mega-event is not only about showing a city off to the world, but it is also about putting the global on show for the locals (especially in the case of marginal cities, see Whitson, 2004). Mega-events thus invite them to take on new identities as citizens of the world (Whitson and Horne, 2006). After a mega-event has finished, questions start to be raised about the popular belief that sport can have a positive impact on a local community and a regional economy. Sport has been seen as a generator of national and local economic and social development. Economically it has been viewed as an industry around which cities can devise urban regeneration strategies. Socially it has been viewed as a tool for the development of urban communities, and the reduction of social exclusion and crime. Whilst hypothetical links exist between sport activities/facilities and work productivity, health, self-esteem, quality of life, employment, and other variables, not as much rigorous research has been done as might be expected given the claims made. Often research has been conducted in advance of sports mega-events on behalf of interested parties. There has been inadequate measurement of final and intermediate outputs as well as inputs.[5]

Our analysis of sports policy and sport infrastructure in Japan over the past twenty years has outlined the changing role of public policy, the new faces of public private partnerships, and the impact of global sports on Japan (Horne and Manzenreiter, 2004; Manzenreiter and Horne, 2005). In the 1990s hundreds of cities, towns and villages announced 'sport' or 'health city' declarations in order to re-brand their local image and to fight rural migration and industrial decline. The hosting of sports mega-events such as the Football World Cup Finals provide multiple meanings for different groups of agents — as they happen, when they have taken place and, perhaps especially, as they are being bid for. Advocates of hosting mega events will deploy a range of discursive strategies to win over public opinion internally.

In the case of semi-peripheral or developing societies, colonial and neo-colonial ties have shaped and continue to shape external relationships with sports mega-events as well. Neither the continents of Africa nor South America have staged an Olympic Games. The unsuccessful bid by Cape Town to host the 2004 Olympic Games was the first African bid for the Games (Swart and Bob 2004). Cornelissen (2004) notes how 'Africa' was used ideologically by both South Africa and Morocco during the competition to host the 2010 Football World Cup that was eventually resolved in favour of the former in May 2004. The South African bid estimated massive benefits from the event, which many consider will be impossible to actually achieve[6]. In the final bid twelve locations were named as sites to host matches, but as in Japan and Korea in 2002 there will be several of these that under-utilise the facilities built and therefore will not obtain the benefits promised.

Megaprojects can be delivered on time and within budget — the Guggenheim Bilbao Museum, the Pompidou Centre, and even further back the Empire State Building and the Eiffel Tower are examples of this (Flyvbjerg, 2005). But the vast majority of megaprojects are not delivered anywhere nearly on time or to their budget (*The Economist*, 11 June 2005: pp. 65–66). It is becoming so evident that cost overruns are predictable that certain sections of government, as well as academics, have begun to consider this more seriously. The Department for Transport in the UK for example commissioned Bent Flyvbjerg to investigate procedures for dealing with, in classic British understatement, "optimism bias" in transport planning (Flyvbjerg, 2004). The UK Government strategy for sport, published in December 2002 by the Department for Culture, Media and Sport, also appeared more cautious about the benefits of hosting sports mega-events following a number of well-publicised failures in recent years. This caution seems to have been forgotten in the bidding process for the 2012 Olympics, possibly because politicians develop a "monument complex". One of the concerns that must be on the minds of the UK population still to be convinced about the 2012 Olympics is whether monuments can turn into white elephants and end up costing more than they are worth to maintain. These are just a few of the unacceptable ideas that are rendered unconscious, or repressed, the 'unknown knowns', or anxieties, surrounding sports mega-events.

Conclusion

It is a great achievement to bring any event together. It is a marvellous feeling to see plans materialise and things come together after months and sometimes years of planning. Hence the response to the announcement on 6 July in London and other parts of the UK contained almost the full gamut of emotions. Sports mega-events promise (albeit brief) moments of "festive intercultural celebration" (Kidd, 1992a: p. 151). But mega-events are very seductive. As was witnessed barely 24 hours later there are other issues that can intrude and burst the Olympic bubble[7].

We can summarise the discussion by stating that sports mega-events are a significant part of the experience of modernity, but they cannot be seen as a panacea for its social and economic problems. Hence there is a need to maintain an independent position to assess these events. As Flyvbjerg suggests the key weapons against a culture of covert deceit surrounding megaprojects are transparency, accountability and critical questioning from independent and specialist organizations. Rather than simply become cheerleaders for them, boosters, rather than analysts, academics need to reflect critically on the effects, beyond economic impacts, that sports mega-events have. As former Olympian Bruce Kidd (1992b: pp. 154) has argued "Mega projects like the Olympic Games require a tremendous investment of human, financial and physical resources from the communities that stage them". They are, as a result, very properly the subject of public debate, not least because they "illuminate competing notions of the public good" (Kidd, 1992b: pp. 154).

Notes

1   These issues include centre–periphery relationships related to governance in world sport (Sugden and Tomlinson, 2002), power relations between nation states, supranational sport associations and the sports business (Butler, 2002), the media–sport–business connection (Jennings with Sambrook, 2000), and the cultural production of ideologies needed to cover emergent fissures when "the circus comes to town" (Horne and Manzenreiter 2004). A substantially revised version of this paper is to be published in *Leisure Studies*.

2   The Winter Olympic Games is roughly one-quarter the size of the Summer Games in terms of athletes and events and so some might argue that it is not a true 'mega' (Matheson and Baade, 2003). Along with the UEFA European Football Championships it certainly qualifies as a 'second order' major international sports event.

3   Between 1980 and 2000 seven new sports and 80 events were added to the programme of the Summer Olympics. 28 sports currently feature in the Summer Olympics. In 1998 the FIFA World Cup Finals expanded from 24 to 32 football teams.

4   Such was the outcry about the spiralling costs associated with the building of the new Scottish Parliament building at Holyrood in

Edinburgh that an inquiry was established. Originally estimated at between £10 and £40 million in the devolution legislation passed in 1997, costs rose to £55 million (1998), £109 million (1999), £195 million (2000) and £374 million (2003). The building was finally opened in 2004 at a cost of £431 million (www.holyrood inquiry.org).

5   One of the main problems regarding the assessment of the costs and benefits of mega events relates to the quality of data obtained from impact analyses. Economic impact studies often claim to show that the investment of public money is worthwhile in the light of the economic activity generated by having professional sports teams or mega events in cities. Yet here much depends on predictions of expenditure by sports tourists. Research shows that such studies have often been methodologically flawed. The real economic benefit of visitor numbers and spending is often well below that specified because of 'substitution', 'crowding out' and unrealistic use of the economic 'multiplier' factors. Another measure of economic impact — on the creation of new jobs in the local economy — has often been politically driven to justify the expenditure on new facilities (see Matheson and Baade, 2003).

6   77,400 permanent jobs, income of 2 per cent of South Africa's GDP and additional income from tax of US$ 550 million (Cornelissen, 2004: p. 1297).

7   Four bomb blasts in central London on 7 July 2005 ('7/7') killed 54 people and injured hundreds the day after London was surprisingly selected to host the 2012 Summer Olympic Games.

References

Baade, R. and Matheson, V. (2002) 'Bidding for the Olympics: Fool's gold?', in C. Barros, M. Ibrahimo and S. Szymanski (eds) *Transatlantic sport*. London: Edward Elgar, pp. 127–151.

Bauman, Z. (1998) *Globalization.* Cambridge: Polity.

Black, D. and van der Westhuizen, J. (2004) 'The allure of global games for 'semi-peripheral', polities and spaces: A research agenda', *Third World Quarterly* Vol. 25, No. 7: pp. 1195–1214.

Butler, O. (2002) 'Getting the Games: Japan, South Korea and the co-hosted World Cup', in J Horne and W Manzenreiter (eds) *Japan, Korea and the 2002 World Cup*. London: Routledge, pp. 43–55.

Cashman, R. (2003) *Impact of the Games on Olympic host cities*. Centre d' Estudis Olimpics, Universitat Autónoma de Barcelona.

Coakley, J. and Donnelly, P. (2004) *Sports in society*. Toronto: McGraw-Hill Ryerson.

Cornelissen, S. (2004) '"It's Africa's turn!"': The narratives and legitimations surrounding the Moroccan and South African bids for the 2006 and 2010 FIFA finals', *Third World Quarterly* Vol. 25, No. 7: pp. 1293–1309.

Crompton, J. (2001) 'Public subsidies to professional team sport facilities in the USA', in C. Gratton and I. Henry (eds) *Sport in the city*. London: Routledge, pp. 15–34.

Flyvbjerg, B. (2005) 'Design by deception: The politics of megaproject approval', *Harvard Design Magazine* No. 22: pp. 50–59.

Flyvbjerg, B. in association with COWI (2004) *Procedures for dealing with optimism bias in transport planning*. London: Department for Transport.

Flyvbjerg, B., Bruzelius, N. and Rothengatter, W. (2003) *Megaprojects and risk*. Cambridge: Cambridge University Press.

Gratton, C. and Henry, I. (eds) *Sport in the city*. London: Routledge.

Hall, C. M. (2001) 'Imaging, tourism and sports event fever: The Sydney Olympics and the need for a social charter for mega-events', in: C. Gratton and I. Henry (eds)*Sport in the city*. pp. 166–183.

Hannigan, J. (1998) *Fantasy City* London: Routledge.

Harvey, D. (1989) *The Condition of Postmodernity* Oxford: Blackwell.

Hoberman, J. (1995) 'Toward a theory of Olympic internationalism', *Journal of Sport History* Vol. 22, No. 1: pp. 1–37.

Horne, J. and Manzenreiter, W. (2004) 'Accounting for mega-events: Forecast and actual impacts of the 2002 Football World Cup Finals on the host countries Japan and Korea', *International Review for the Sociology of Sport* Vol. 39, No. 2: pp. 187–203.

Hughes, R. (1992) *Barcelona*. New York: A. Knopf.

Jessop, B. (2002) *The future of the capitalist state*. Cambridge: Polity.

Katwala, S. (2000) *Democratising global sport*. London: Foreign Policy Centre.

Kidd, B. (1992a) 'The culture wars of the Montreal Olympics', *International Review for the Sociology of Sport* Vol. 27, No.2: pp. 151–161.

Kidd, B. (1992b) 'The Toronto Olympic Commitment: Towards a Social Contract for the Olympic Games', *Olympika* Vol. 1, No.1: 154–167.

Krüger, A. (1993) Book review of J. Boix and A. Espada *El deporte del poder: vida y milagro de Juan Antonio Samaranch.* (Madrid: Ediciones temas de hoy, 1991).

Lenskyj, H. (2004) 'The Olympic Industry and Civil Liberties: The Threat to Free Speech and Freedom of Assembly', *Sport in Society* Vol. 7, No. 3: pp. 370–384.

Lenskyj, H. (2002) *The Best Olympics ever? Social impacts of Sydney 2000* Albany, NY: SUNY Press.

Lenskyj, H. (2000) *Inside the Olympic Industry* Albany, NY: SUNY Press.

Lenskyj, H. (1998) 'Sport and corporate environmentalism', *International Review for the Sociology of Sport* Vol. 33, No. 4: pp. 341–354.

Lenskyj, H. (1996) 'When winners are losers: Toronto and Sydney bids for the Summer Olympics', *Journal of Sport and Social Issues* Vol. 24, No. 4: pp. 392–410.

Manzenreiter, W. and Horne, J. (2005) 'Public policy, sports investments and regional development initiatives in contemporary Japan', in J. Nauright and K. Schimmel (eds) *The political economy of sport.* London: Palgrave

Matheson, V. and Baade, R. (2003) 'Mega-sporting events in developing nations: Playing the way to prosperity?', unpublished paper.

Nauright, J. (2004) 'Global games: Culture, political economy and sport in the globalised world of the 21st century', *Third World Quarterly* 25(7): pp. 1325–1336.

Roberts, K. (2004) *The leisure industries.* London: Palgrave.

Roche, M. (2000) *Mega-events and modernity.* London: Routledge.

Rumsfeld, D. (n.d.) www.bbc.co.uk/radio4/news/bh/rumsfeld.shtml.

Sugden, J. and Tomlinson, A. (2002) 'International power struggles in the governance of world football: The 2002 and 2006 World Cup bidding wars', In J. Horne and W. Manzenreiter (eds) *Japan, Korea and the 2002 World Cup,* pp. 56–70.

Swart, K. and Bob, U. (2004) 'The seductive discourse of development: The Cape Town 2004 Olympic bid', *Third World Quarterly* Vol. 25, No. 7: pp. 1311–1324.

UK Sport (1999) *Measuring success.* London: UK Sport.

UK Sport (2004) *Measuring success 2.* London: UK Sport.

Pickup By: 2/11/2010

Zhao

74013

Sporting events and event tourism : impacts, plans and opportunities

Vázquez Montalbán, M. (1990/1992) *Barcelonas.* London: Verso.

—— (1991/2004) *An Olympic death.* London: Serpent',s Tail.

Vigor, A., Mean, M. and Tims, C. (eds) (2004) *After the Gold Rush: A sustainable Olympics for London.* London: Institute for Public Policy Research (IPPR)/Demos.

Whitson, D. (2004) 'Bringing the world to Canada: 'The periphery of the centre', *Third World Quarterly* Vol. 25, No. 7: pp. 1215–1232.

Whitson, D. (1998) 'Circuits of promotion: Media, marketing and the globalization of sport', in L. Wenner (ed) *MediaSport.* London: Routledge, pp. 57-72.

Whitson, D. and Horne, J. (2006) 'Underestimated costs and overestimated benefits? Comparing the outcomes of sports mega-events in Canada and Japan', in J. Horne and W. Manzenreiter (eds) *Sports mega-events.* Oxford: Blackwell/ Sociological Review Monograph series.

Wilson, H. (1996) 'What is an Olympic city? Visions of Sydney 2000', *Media, Culture and Society* Vol. 18, No. 3: pp. 603–618.

Zizek, S. (2005) 'The empty wheelbarrow', *The Guardian* 19 February, p. 23.

STAGING THE CRICKET WORLD CUP 2007 IN THE CARIBBEAN: ISSUES AND CHALLENGES FOR SMALL ISLAND DEVELOPING STATES

Leslie-Ann Jordan

Department of Management Studies
University of the West Indies, Trinidad, West Indies

This paper examines the Cricket World Cup 2007, which will be held in the Caribbean from February to April 2007. For the first time in any sport, a World Cup is to be staged in eight (8) independent countries, each with its own government, flag and anthem. None of the Caribbean territories hosting a match has a population larger than Jamaica's 3.4 million; most have less than quarter of a million people. Economies are small and infrastructure limited. Utilizing interviews and secondary research, the main aim of this paper is to examine the major challenges and issues faced by these small island developing states (SIDS) as they attempt to host the single biggest sporting event ever in the Caribbean, which is already being called a "logistical nightmare" by some. More specifically, the key issues to be analyzed include: regional co-ordination and co-operation; challenges with the free movement of people and border control between the islands; the ability of the islands to accommodate and service an estimated 100,000 visitors; safety and security and; strategies to maximize public and private sector involvement. The paper will also examine the institutional arrangements and logistical procedures that have been designed to help manage the expected economic, socio-cultural and political impacts of this mega-event. Additionally, it will also document some of the critical success factors that will help determine the overall success of the event.

Introduction

Mega sports events such as the Olympic games, the football World Cup or the Cricket World Cup have been highly sought after commodities by countries and cities throughout the world. These events are viewed as powerful tools for both stimulating economic development, as well as gaining international recognition (Hall, 1992; Andranovish *et al.*, 2001; Burbank *et al.*, 2002). Over the past two decades, sports, and the hosting of mega sports events, has assumed a greater role in the economies of developing countries as they attempt to regenerate regional, national and local identities within the globalization process (Holder, 2003; John, 2004). While major sporting events still cater to a core fan base, most organizers realize the market for sporting events has broadened considerably and that many visitors are as interested in the destination as the event itself (Hall, 1992; Emery, 2002).

Most events now borrow from the Olympics event model, incorporating entertainment, culture and other activities that highlight the destination's culture and heritage knowing that today's tourists often use a hallmark or special event as a motivation to visit a new destination. The term "Hallmark Event" now commonly refers to "a recurring event that possesses such significance, in terms of tradition, attractiveness, image, or publicity, that the event provides the host venue, community, or destination with a competitive advantage (Getz, 1997: p. 5).

Traditionally, the emphasis of these major events has focused on revitalizing urban centers through the creation of new facilities (e.g. stadiums), improvements to the infrastructure (e.g., transportation and hotels), and an increase in tourism revenues (Hall, 1992; Emery, 2002). However, governments and organizers now recognize that these events can have significant impacts on areas outside of the urban center. Many researchers agree that sports tourism can produce significant socio-cultural benefits such as promoting and preserving local culture and identity through the involvement of local communities in the development of events, products and activities (Hall, 1992; Getz, 1997; Andranovish *et al.*, 2001; Burbank *et al.*, 2002; Holder, 2003; Waitt, 2003).

For the first time in the history of the International Cricket Council World Cup (ICC CWC), the event will be hosted by the West Indies (see Figure 1). The ICC CWC West Indies 2007 (ICC CWC WI 2007) comprises a record sixteen (16) teams set to contest 51 matches, including 24 first-round games, 24 matches in the Super Eight stage, two Semi-finals and the Final. It will officially begin on March 13, 2007 in Jamaica and will end on April 28, 2007 at Kensington Oval, Barbados. It is expected that the World Cup will be seen by over 1.4 billion around the globe, over five continents, by at least 10 international broadcasters (30).

Whether or not these benefits can be realized depends largely on the necessary work being done in a planned and co-coordinated manner between all the stakeholders involved.

According to Donald Lockerbie, the Venue Development Director, "There is no blueprint for putting on a World Cup in nine countries! Nobody has ever done it before!" (Campbell, 2005). Given this background, the main objective of this paper is to examine the major challenges and issues faced by these small island developing states (SIDS) as they attempt to host the single biggest sporting event ever in the Caribbean, which is already being called a "logistical nightmare" by some. More specifically, the paper will document the procedure used to determine which islands will be used as host venues. It will also discuss some of the key issues facing the region, such as: challenges with the free movement of people and border control between the islands; the ability of the islands to accommodate and service an estimated 100,000 visitors; safety and security and; strategies to maximize public and private sector involvement. The paper will also examine the institutional arrangements and logistical procedures that have been designed to help manage the expected economic, socio-cultural and political impacts of this mega-event. Additionally, it will also explore specific strategies that are being developed to ensure that the World Cup helps to bolster the region's tourism industry.

The information for this paper was drawn from multiple secondary sources, including: local government documents, official documents, media reports, national and regional newspapers, Internet resources and other available sources (e.g. speeches, papers, press releases and presentations).

Institutional arrangements

This mega-event requires a regional effort and there are several key stakeholders involved in the event management process: the International Cricket Council (ICC); the West Indies Cricket Board (WICB);

the Caribbean Community (CARICOM); National Governments; the ICC CWC WI 2007 Inc.; the eight Local Organizing Committees (LOC); National Tourist Boards and; the general public.

The regional planning and management of the World Cup is being conducted by the ICC CWC WI 2007 Inc., which is the company set up by the WICB to manage and deliver the event (*Guyana Chronicle*, 2003a). Headquartered in Jamaica, the ICC CWC WI 2007 Inc. operates as a separate entity and its main responsibility is to "plan and deliver a seamless World Cup that will bring honour and economic benefit to the Caribbean, not only for the World Cup but long after" (*Barbados Nation Newspaper*, 2004). More specifically, their vision statement is:

> To execute the hosting of the ICC Cricket world Cup West Indies 2007 to world class standards in order to achieve the operational requirements and economic and strategic objectives of the WICB and the ICC, in a manner which enhances the international reputation and prestige of the Caribbean and specifically, West Indies Cricket.

The ICC CWC WI 2007 Inc. has listed eight key objectives of the event:

1. High Quality Event Management – to demonstrate indisputably to the world the Caribbean's capacity to successfully plan and execute a world class event, specifically world class cricket, and to develop supporting facilities worthy of a global event
2. Brand Legacy – to ensure an enduring, positive emotional association with the ICC Cricket World Cup 2007 by the international and Caribbean cricketing community
3. Infrastructure Improvement – to make permanent improvement to the sporting and general country infrastructure in the Caribbean
4. Widespread Economic Opportunity – to facilitate a widespread, equitable and fair participation in the economic opportunities of the event
5. Unique Caribbean Promotion – to promote a unified Caribbean as a premier business and tourist destination for all the world's nationalities
6. Regional Integration – to advance the process of regional integration
7. High Profitability – to maximize profitability to WICB and member territories so as to secure the foundation for West Indies cricket development, before and after the ICC Cricket World Cup 2007

8. Enhance the International Popularity of Cricket – to meet the ICC's objective of raising the international profile of the glorious game in the Caribbean, the Hemisphere and the world

The ICC CWC WI 2007 Inc. has sought to keep the leaders of CARICOM fully informed and involved by partnering with the CARICOM Prime Ministerial Sub-Committee on Cricket, chaired by Grenada's Prime Minister, Dr. Keith Mitchell. They have recognized that it is principally with CARICOM'S assistance that they would be able to develop world class venues, grounds and practice facilities as well as stage world class opening and closing ceremonies; provide high quality accommodation for participating teams and visitors; put in place appropriate legislation to protect commercial rights; and implement security and anti-terrorism strategies (WICB, 2004a).

At the country level, the planning and management of country-based activities have been designated to LOCs, which report directly to their respective Governments, as well as to the ICC CWC WI 2007.

Venue selection process

In order to assist the WICB with assessing venues for the allocation of matches, the ICC CWC WI 2007 Inc. used an Olympic style bidding process to determine the venues. The term "venue" in this case referred to, not just one small geographic area within a country, but to the entire country. In order to select the host venues for the competition, a five-step process was followed:

1) Develop venue development blueprint — the Bid Book
2) Countries applied or 'bid' to host matches
3) Independent technical assessment by Venue Assessment Team (VAT)
4) Matches awarded
5) Contracting and monitoring to ensure compliance

Bid Book

This is the first time in the history of the ICC CWC that a Bid Book had to be developed. The Bid Book was developed to ensure that any Caribbean country could make its bid to be a host venue with the full knowledge of the detailed technical, operational and legal requirements. The

Bid Book was the culmination of months of collaboration between ICC CWC 2007 Inc., the Venue Assessment Team (VAT), the ICC and Global Cricket Corporation. According to Chris Dehring, Managing Director and Chief Executive Officer (CEO) of the ICC WI CWC 2007 Inc., the 300-page Bid Book was designed to "prepare potential host venues for events of this scale and facilitate selection in a professional, fair and transparent manner" (WICB, 2004b; WICB, 2004c). The Book outlined 24 deliverables, which venues had to be able to achieve to world-class standards. These deliverables included:

1) Cricket stadia
2) Match day operations
3) Cricket grounds
4) Security issues
5) Medical facilities
6) Spectator facilities
7) Finance
8) Accommodation
9) Political environment
10) Local organizing committee
11) Disaster management
12) Media facilities
13) Accreditation
14) Communications
15) Marketing support
16) Immigration and customs operations
17) Host venue agreement and related legal issues
18) Transport
19) WICB Rights/Sponsor Contractual Obligations
20) Climate and environment
21) Ambush marketing
22) Generic event functions
23) Economic impact assessment
24) Bid commitment and guarantees (WCSL, 2004; WICB, 2004a)

In an attempt to ensure national support, bid submissions required the endorsement of both the national cricket association, as well as the respective Government, in order to be accepted. As is the case with other international sporting events such as the Commonwealth Games, FIFA World Cup and the Olympics, host venues will be required to execute the terms and conditions laid out in a binding host venue agreement, which is a requirement of the ICC.

In total, twelve countries submitted bids: Antigua and Barbuda, Bahamas, Bermuda, Cayman Islands, Guyana, Grenada, Jamaica, Trinidad and Tobago, St. Lucia, St. Vincent and the Grenadines, St Kitts and Nevis and the United States. These countries were then visited by the Venue Assessment Team (VAT).

Venue Assessment Team (VAT)

The Venue Assessment Team, which is an independent body of inter-national experts who have prior experience in World Championships and Cricket World Cup, assessed each bid. Between May 24 and June 11, 2004, they visited each country that submitted a bid in order to understand first hand the strengths of each ground and examine the challenges that some venues face (*Trinidad Express*, 2004; WICB, 2004d). After this process was completed, the VAT reported the findings and recommendations to the ICC CWC WI 2007 Inc., which then made the allocations of matches that was sent to the ICC for approval.

Finally, eight tournament venues were announced: Antigua and Barbuda, Barbados, Grenada, Guyana, Jamaica, St. Lucia, St. Kitts and Nevis and Trinidad and Tobago. These countries are all considered small island developing states (SIDS) and they are sovereign countries, each with its own government, flag and anthem. None of the Caribbean territories hosting a match has a population larger than Jamaica's 3.4 million; most have less than quarter of a million people. Economies are small and infrastructure limited (see Table 1).

Allocation matrix

During the World Cup, the West Indies, Australia, India and England will be placed in four separate groups during the opening stages of the Cup (see Table 2). Organizers have justified this grouping by stating, "the placement of teams has been designed in an attempt to give a fair breakdown of not just high-quality cricket matches, but give the venues where the matches will be played, a chance to maximize on the fan support of the four countries" (WICB, 2004e). According to Dehring, "We want to spread the ICC World Cup Windies 2007 to as wide a constituent as possible because it is our obligation to this region to make sure that the economic benefits of this is felt by everybody in the regionÖ" (WICB, 2004e).

Teams, matches and events for the Cup have been categorized in a multi-coloured allocation matrix. As Table 2 shows, there were eight packages awarded.

Table 3 shows the timeline for the entire venue selection process.

Table 1   Profile of Host Countries

	Area (sq. km)	Population	GDP (US$ million)	Tourist Arrivals (000's)
Antigua & Barbuda	440	71,800	459	236.7
Barbados	431	267,500	2,154	544.7
Grenada	344	101,700	256	128.9
Guyana	216,000	772,200	569	105.0
Jamaica	11,424	2.6 million	6,271	1,322.7
St. Lucia	616	156,000	434	269.9
St. Kitts & Nevis	269	40,400	207	73.1
Trinidad & Tobago	5,128	1.3 million	5,927	398.2

Source: CTO, 2001

Table 2   Allocation Matrix for CWC 2007

Country	Package	Cricket Team	Venue
Jamaica	*Yellow package*—the Opening ceremony, the Opening Game, the Semi-final and six first round matches	West Indies base	*Sabina Park* Capacity: 16,000 CWC: 30,000 After event: 20,000
St. Lucia	*Blue package* – the other Semi-final and six first round matches	England's base	*Beausejour Stadium* Capacity: 12,000. CWC: 21,000
St. Kitts and Nevis	*Orange package* – six first round matches	Australia's base	*Warner Park Stadium* Capacity: 4,000. CWC: 10,000
Trinidad and Tobago	*Brown package* – six first round matches (12)	India's base	*Queen's Park Oval* Capacity: 25,000 CWC:
Barbados	*Black package* – Six Super Eight/quarter-final matches including three of the biggest Super Eight matches, Final		*Kensington Oval* Capacity: 32, 000
Antigua and Barbuda	*Red package*—Six Super Eight/quarter-final matches including three of the biggest Super Eight matches		*Sir Vivian Richards Stadium*—new venue Capacity: 20,000 of which 10,000 will be permanent
Grenada	*Green One*—Six Super Eight/quarter-final matches		*Queen's Park* Capacity: 13,000 CWC: 20,000
Guyana	*Green Two* – Six Super Eight/quarter-final matches (21)(37)(38)		*Providence Stadium,* new venue Capacity: 20,000

Table 3   Timeline for Venue Selection Process

Date	Activity
February 19, 2004	Bid books handed over to representatives of the 13 registered Bid Committee
March 10, 2004	Letters of intent submitted to ICC CWC Windies 2007 Inc.
May 6, 2004	Bids submitted to ICC CWC WI 2007 Inc.
May 24 to June 13, 2004	VAT visits each country that submitted a bid
July 4, 2004	Venues/countries announced
July 13, 2004	Awarding of matches

Challenges of hosting the Cricket World Cup 2007

It is predicted that the 2007 World Cup will attract an unprecedented number of visitors to the Caribbean, spending more money and time than the current tourist. More than 100,000 visitors, not counting returning Caribbean residents from the United States, Britain and Canada, are expected in the region for a six-week period. They are expected to spend about US $250 million on accommodation, transportation, entertainment, food and beverages and souvenirs. Given these predictions, there are several challenges to hosting this event such as:

- Accommodation
- Transportation
- Customs and Immigration
- Security and Safety
- Public awareness and public participation
- Ambush marketing and other legal issues
- Ticketing and hospitality package logistics
- Managing event impacts

This paper, while addressing all of these challenges, will discuss transportation and accommodation in greater detail as they are considered the two biggest challenges that will affect the smooth running of the CWC 2007.

Accommodation

There are approximately 46,000 hotel rooms in the entire English- speaking Caribbean (WICB, 2002) and the CWC is expected to draw about

Table 4   Accommodation supply in Host Venues – CWC 2007

Countries	Number of rooms
Antigua & Barbuda	3,185
Barbados	6,456
Grenada	1,822
Guyana	730
Jamaica	23,640
St. Lucia	4,525
St. Kitts & Nevis	2,029
Trinidad & Tobago	4,532
TOTAL	46,919

Table 5   Accommodation supply for Host Venues by room type – CWC 2007

	Antigua & Barbuda	Barbados	Grenada	Guyana	Jamaica	St. Lucia	St. Kitts & Nevis	Trinidad & Tobago	TOTAL ROOMS
Hotels	2,963	1,942	1,197		16,110	2,801	1,503	2,672	
Apart-ment Hotels		2,309							
Apart-ment/ Cottages		2,019	393				275		
Apart-ments	168				1,381	1,201			
Guest Houses	54	186	232		2,417	523	251	945	
Resort Lodge				86					
Hotel/ Guest House				644					
Resort Cottages					3,732				
Condos								471	
Other								444	
TOTAL ROOMS	3,185	6,456	1,822	730	23,640	4,525	2,029	4,532	46,919

Source: CTO, 2001

100,000 visitors to the region (see Tables 4 and 5). The seriousness of the accommodation challenge can be understood by examining the following scenario — if you were to take all the hotel rooms in the entire Caribbean and put them in Barbados, Barbados would still be stretched to host a hypothetical match between England and India.For example, in St. Lucia they have acknowledged that there is a need to increase the island's hotel room capacity from 4,500 to about 7,500. In order to accomplish this, the St. Lucian government has announced a special package of incentives for new developments or expansions of properties completed before December 31, 2006 (*Guyana Chronicle*, 2004a). Other host venues have also employed similar strategies to help address the huge deficit between accommodation demand and supply.

There have been several solutions offered to try to accommodate the thousands expected for the Competition (CTO, 2005; WICB, 2005f). Some of these include:

- Housing visitors in private homes — this would allow visitors to experience Caribbean culture and culinary skills up close and personal. However, stringent standards must be developed and implemented before private homes can be deemed suitable for international travelers
- Designating official team hotels
- Using Cruise ships as 'floating hotels'
- Using bed and breakfast homes
- Using off island accommodation – yachts
- Accommodating people in one country and transporting them to another on a daily basis for games of their choice.

Freedom of movement — transportation, customs and immigration

Freedom of movement within each country, as well as between islands will be a critical success factor for the event. Sixteen (16) teams have to be housed and moved from match to match over a five-week period. So too, do the attendant media and the tens of thousands of disparate supporters. According to one sports journalist, "for anyone who has to endure the long lines, perennial delays and incidents of lost luggage every season when there is just one visiting team in the Caribbean, the consequences of thousands of fun-loving but impatient fans traveling through the region are almost frightening" (Mohammed, 2005: p. 53).

Given this situation, the burning question has been — How will all these visitors move through the Caribbean and within the venue, given the fact that it is often difficult for regional media workers to travel hassle-free through airports while covering regional competitions? (Devers, 2003). Given the expected capacity and the fact that most of the inter-island aircrafts can only carry fifty passengers at one time, it will be necessary to conduct flights throughout the night for some games, as well as to wet lease some aircrafts, charter others and even use international flights. However, the existing aviation laws in the Caribbean does not allow an aircraft registered in the United States or Europe to fly between Caribbean countries. Therefore, hosting a successful event will necessitate a relaxing of those laws in order to allow foreign pilots to come into the region and fly for that period. It will also require that all facilities at designated airports (such as air traffic control, immigration, customs, baggage handling and security) must be open all night (Hosein, 2005; Street, 2005). The ICC CWC WI 2007 Inc. has attempted to alleviate some of the inter-island traffic by scheduling games three to four days apart and keeping the "Super Eight" games relatively within the Eastern Caribbean countries. Compounding this issue is the fact that inter-island ferry services barely exist and the three main regional airlines, BWIA, LIAT and Air Jamaica have been experiencing major financial and operational difficulties (Cozier, 2004; Wilkinson, 2004).

Another major related challenge is customs and immigration. Those who travel through the region for the World Cup will have to deal with different immigration and customs procedures in each territory and make at least five currency changes at contrasting exchange rates (eg. Barbadian dollar, Eastern Currency, Guyanese dollar, Jamaican dollar and the Trinidad & Tobago dollar) (Cozier, 2004; Vice, 2005). The members of CARICOM, along with the ICC CWC WI 2007 Inc., have committed themselves to issuing one World Cup "passport" to media and fans throughout the tournament to loosen possible ties of red tape. Other plans include:

- Special system for processing for Teams and Officials
- Once only immigration processing – machine readable cards
- Electronic processing: World Cup passport
- Visa fee waived
- Departure tax waived

Additionally, sunset legislation is currently being drafted in con-sultation with CARICOM and the Attorney Generals of the host countries and is expected to address the movement of people and equipment for the duration of the event.

Ticketing and hospitality

Cricket Logistics 2007 was chosen as the Official Tour Operator for the event. They are a consortium made up of Gullivers Sports Travel, UK and Hospitality in Partnership UK. Gullivers will handle all aspects of travel while Hospitality in Partnership will deal with all facets of match-day hospitality. They will be the sole source of commercial tickets that are sold as part of a tour and travel or hospitality package for the event. They will also mange all travel and accommodation arrangements for participating teams, official and event sponsors, as well as providing for media (WICB, 2005a; WICB, 2005b). As Official Tour operator, they are mandated to appoint a worldwide network of Official Travel Agents (OTA), through public tender process, in consultation with ICC CWC WI 2007 Inc. These OTAs will be responsible for the sale of official supporters' packages, consisting of travel, accommodation and match tickets for overseas supporters (WICB, 2005b).

However, there is some discontent amongst accommodation pro-viders in the region concerning the monopoly that Cricket Logistics has. In addition to booking lodging, attractions and transportation, Cricket Logistics is also reserving large blocks of airline tickets and event tickets for these packages. They have also requested that hotels reserve a large percentage of their rooms for their packages but there is some resistance among members of the Hotels Associations in the region, due in large part to the lack of information concerning how these arrangements will be governed. Hoteliers have argued that they will not turn down their regular guests — and in the case of Trinidad and Tobago, their Carnival bookings — until they are assured by Cricket Logistics that they will be adequately compensated. Some hoteliers have also voiced their concern about the fact that if they do not work through Cricket Logistics, they risk not being able to obtain event tickets for their guests.

Security and safety issues

In the global climate of terrorist attacks, the issue of security is of enor-mous importance, as well as health care and emergency services. Some authors have noted that in the Caribbean, there is a general indifference to safety and security issues and so the greatest challenge will perhaps be in trying to educate the general public concerning the new 'rules' that would be put in place for the event. For example, it may be a bit of a culture shock when the World Cup comes around and fans who have been accustomed to parking close to the venue or taking in their ice coolers filled with drinks are told that they can no longer do so (Mohammed, 2005). Although people are more aware of their personal safety, it will still take a special effort of the LOCs' part to get them to accept repeated searches at various points entering the venues, as well as again upon entering.

The security and safety of visiting Teams and Officials is also paramount. In the past, teams such as Australia, Sri Lanka and even the West Indies, have complained about missing items from their bags as they passed through the Caribbean ports, as well as the late arrival of luggage and gear (Devers, 2003; WICB, 2003a). In order to ensure the readiness of the region, senior representatives from the police force of all eight (8) participating countries have started to receive training on the role and function of security in the execution of an international mega event (ICC, 2005a). A Security Directorate Seminar held in May 2005 covered issues including emergency evacuation, stadium access, crowd control and anti-social behaviour (Stabroek News, 2004).

Community participation and involvement

The CEO of the ICC CWC WI 2007 Inc. has said that one of the most challenging tasks ahead is to make the people of the Caribbean understand that "what we are talking about is the ICC World CupÖthis is not the West Indies' World Cup to do what we want and to any standards we choose" (WICB, 2002b). Many authors have also noted that the more difficult task to accomplish may be the education of the public over sponsors' rights and ambush marketing (Cozier, 2004). For example, West Indians feel it is their right to swig their Mount Gay Rum, Carib Beer or Red Strip Beer in the venue but in 2007, it will have to be the booze of the sponsor who has spent millions to have its brand associated with the event. If the general public is not fully educated about these issues and if they do not accept the terms of engagement, then multi-million dollar lawsuits are imminent if one country lets down the rest of the region (*Guyana Chronicle*, 2003b).

The *ICC World Cup Cricket West Indies 2007 Act*, which is the legislation to govern the event should be drafted and enacted by the middle of 2005 and become fully operational across the region by the end of 2006. For example, this Act will dictate that Kensington Oval in Barbados and its environs will have to be absolutely "clean" of all signage in order for it to be usable as an official stadium (WICB, 2002b). The Act also addresses a range of issues including security, customs and immigration matters, ambush marketing, taxation, events management and other operational aspects of the World Cup. Additionally, the ICC CWC WI 2007 Inc. has managed to secure US $100 million of insurance for the event from the international insurance market (WICB, 2005c).

Opportunities for hosting Cricket World Cup 2007

Major sports events have the potential to offer significant benefits to any city or destination and the CWC 2007 is no different. To date, much has already been published about the potential benefits of hosting the CWC 2007 in the Caribbean, including:

- Generation of new industries and a stimulus for infrastructural development
- Creation of employment
- Creation of government revenue form regulatory fees and taxation
- Increased sports and recreation facilities for local communities leading to improved social interaction
- Creation of other economic benefits as visitors arrive and spend money across the society (WICB, 2002a; Holder, 2003; Pestano, 2003)

Economic benefits

In terms of the economic impacts, there have been several estimates of the potential positive economic impact of the World Cup on the region. Some reports claim that it will gross an estimated US $300 million over the six-week period, generating an estimated US $500 million in direct revenue as a result of the various activities associated with the game and US $750 million in economic activity (*Trinidad Express*, 2004; WICB, 2002a). Other estimates state that Caribbean countries stand to earn about US $600 million over the next three years (2004–2007).(Hines, 2004). In the ICC CWC 2007's Master Plan the measurable goals to achieve economic benefits from the event, include:

- the creation of about 2,000 jobs in each match-playing country;
- the value creation of US$500 million in gross economic impact; and
- external cash inflows of US$300 million (CTO, 2005).

The WICB also stands to earn a hefty sum for staging the event. Andrew Eade, the new International Cricket Council (ICC) Global Development Officer, has disclosed that over a seven-year period, the WICB will earn about US$103 million in television money alone for the month long competition (Davidson, 2002; Spooner, 2003).

In the midst of all these predictions, there are doubts and questions about how much money will actually remain in the periphery. In response to this concern, the ICC CWC WI 2007 inc. has developed the Caribbean Economic Enterprise (CEE) Initiative. The main objective of the CEE is to ensure that the people of the Caribbean benefit from the World Cup, not only economically, but also in terms of knowledge, skills and infrastructure (WICB, 2005a). Under this policy, even if contracts are awarded to non-Caribbean entities through the competitive process, they in turn must develop programmes that will benefit Caribbean companies or nationals and show how nationals will benefit both economically and developmentally. As part of the CEE, the only companies that Cricket Logistics 2007 will deal with in the Caribbean will be of Caribbean origin. As a result, it is predicted that many hotels, bed and breakfasts, ground handlers, guides, bus companies, boast and ships in the region will benefit from CWC 2007. The key to this arrangement working efficiently greatly depends on the strength of the partnerships that Cricket Logistics 2007 is able to build with regional and local Tourist Boards in the Caribbean (WICB, 2005b).

Such engagements or partnerships will facilitate the objectives of empowering persons within the region and leaving a legacy of local persons with the knowledge, understanding and experience of hosting a world-class mega event.

Socio-cultural and political benefits

The upcoming CWC is more than just a mega-event for the Caribbean. It is a platform on which small island developing states with the lingering colonial stigma of 'underdeveloped, third world status' can finally prove to the world that they have the expertise, managerial capacity, resources and wherewithal to plan and deliver a 'first world,

world class' event. The event is being used as a platform to promote the destination and gain positive publicity for the region; elevate national and regional pride and morale; bring together various elements of the society, public and private sector, to work for the common good of the society; and catapult the calls for greater regional integration (Stabroek, 2002; Holder, 2003). According to Edwin Carrington, CARICOM Secretary General, the CWC 2007 can be used as "Öan instrument for grasping opportunities in the globalized world as well as a platform from which to launch the effective integration of the region's economies into the global economy as efficient and competitive players" (*Stabroek News*, 2002, n.p.).

Tourism opportunities

The CWC 2007 is being viewed by the region as a major tourism opportunity. The ICC CWC WI 2007 Inc. has also entered into a partnership with the Caribbean Tourism Organization (CTO) and has established a Tourism Task Force on the ICC Cricket World Cup 2007. The hotel and tourism sector must position itself to take advantage of these benefits and linkages that will be created as a result of hosting the games. These linkages include: construction/renovation of facilities and overall state infrastructure (accommodation, venues, roads, etc.); strengthening the auxiliary and other services; development and promotion of the cultural expressions of the region; marketing of the Caribbean at a global level; strengthening intra-regional linkages at the political and local levels; and increased competitiveness of the Caribbean tourism industry (CTO, 2005).

However, continued negative reports on the Caribbean region could result in the region not being able to fully maximize tourism opportunities. In addition to the service related problems, visitors have also complained about the increase in crime in Guyana, Trinidad and Jamaica and this is another problem that has to be dealt with by the regional governments if the WICB hopes to encourage massive support for the staging of a World Cup in the region.

Private sector involvement

Private sector involvement and support is another critical success factor. The region's financial institutions have been challenged to raise the capital needed for Caribbean businesses to exploit the substantial opportunities being offered by the CWC 2007 (*Stabroek News*, 2003). Business opportunities which will be created by hosting the event could facilitate much more than internal growth for Caribbean businesses by internationally exposing the best of the region's products and services. However, as Dehring emphasized during his presentation to Caribbean bankers in Montego Bay, Jamaica, "This can only happen if the region's financial institutions consciously develop an understanding of the economics of hosting such a global sports event, and mobilize the debt and equity capital needed to expand their clients' businesses to meet the challenge" (*Stabroek News*, 2003, n.p.).

During his presentation, Dehring also noted that not only larger entrepreneurs would need capital but he also argued that, "We must facilitate the small businesses as well and unleash the creative entrepreneurial energy of the region. There will be a need for an increase in virtually every service area from more taxis to increased and varied food supply and Caribbean banks have a responsibility to grow their customers' businesses to take advantage of the opportunities, while at the same time expanding and strengthening their own portfolios" (*Stabroek News*, 2003, n.p.). Businessmen in the region have been challenged to get together with their Caribbean partners within the new CSME to provide on a regional basis, the services, equipment, facilities, accommodation, transportation and other requirements which the organizers would need (*Stabroek News*, 2002).

Infrastructure developments

It is estimated that a total of US $250 million will be spent to build eight new stadiums across the Caribbean in preparation for the matches (Hines, 2004; WICB, 2005d) (see Table 6). Of this, regional governments are expected to spend a total of US $180 million. Generally, the cricket stadiums in the Caribbean are in poor shape (WICB, 2002c). They average around 15,000 in minimal quality seating capacity against an average of 30,000 high quality seating that will be required for 2007. The region has learnt from other countries that have been left with unused mega-structures after hosting mega-events and so additional seating capacity will be constructed in such a way so that the region is not left with the proverbial "white elephants" when the 2007 World Cup is over (WICB, 2002c). Individual host countries will have to invest in their airports, seaports, roadways, hotels, power plants (electricity) and

Table 6   Samples of Infrastructure Costs of the Cricket World Cup 2007

Country	Infrastructure Developments	Estimated costs
Jamaica		US $28 million
St. Kitts	• Upgrade Warner Park	US $15 million
Barbados	• Upgrade Kensington Oval • Modernize highway system	US $90 million
Guyana	• Construct 500 houses that can hold about 8 persons each • Contruct a se cond road to th e Cheddi Jagan International Airport (CJIA) • Upgrade CJIA • Construct international hotels at Liliendaal • Beautify landscape in capital city (51)	US $20 million
Grenada	• Upgrade Queen's Park	US $15 million
Trinidad and Tobago	• Upgrade Queen's Park Oval • Security • Upgrade of roads • Entertainment	US $22 million
St. Lucia		EC $35 million

Sources: CaribbeanCricket.com, 2004; *Trinidad Express*, 2004

internet (broadband) connection speeds, which will have to be on par with the developed world (Pestano, 2003).

However, some of these developments have come with social costs. For example, in Barbados, in order to facilitate the massive restructuring of the Kensington Oval, the government had to acquire houses and relocate local residents surrounding the Oval. Space around the Oval will also be acquired to facilitate improved car parking, practice pitches and the relocation of some stands that may be demolished and upgraded (WICB, 2003b).

Critical success factors

There are a number of critical success factors that will determine the overall success the CWC 2007, including: executive management;

collaboration and communication; community participation and involvement; research and development. The documentation of these critical success factors and their sub-factors is merely a first step in the process of assuring their implementation and making them a permanent part of the event management process. There is also the issue of assuring their effectiveness and use by the appropriate stakeholders who have a vested interest in the success of the CWC 2007.

Critical Success Factor – Executive Management (ICC CWC WI 2007 Inc.)
- Clear prioritization of tasks
- Use accurate data to support actions at all levels of decision-making
- Create accountability for all Committees
- Clarify expectations, roles and responsibilities of all Committees and their members
- Conduct regular reviews to assure and verify progress
- Provide timely information to decision-makers
- Management of critical resources
- Not allowing politicking to interfere with the accomplishment of event goals and objectives

Critical Success Factor – Collaboration and Communication
- At the executive level, collaboration between ICC, CARICOM, WICB and ICC CWC WI 2007 Inc.
- Inter-island collaboration between relevant Ministries and organizations
- Public and Private Sector Partnerships between Government Ministries such as Sports, Tourism, Finance, Culture, Planning and Community Development and private organizations such as financial organizations, Chambers of Commerce and community groups.
- Communication of pertinent facts about CWC to the general public on a regular consistent basis
- Development and dissemination of information

Critical Success Factor — Community participation and involvement
- Ensure the involvement of communities in the decision-making process
- Determine the key role of community tourism

- Public awareness and education – the public's ability to understand and accept the rules of engagement – eg. ambush marketing

Critical Success Factor – Best Practices: Learning from past mistakes
- Research best practices from other destinations that have successfully and unsuccessfully hosted mega-events
- Conduct impact assessments (economic, environmental and socio-cultural) before, during and after the event
- Facilities must be designed with the relevant expert advice
- Awareness of the recurrent operational costs
- Clear and innovative ideas about profit maximization to ensure cost recovery
- Avoid 'white elephants'

Conclusions

This paper attempted to document the essential preliminaries on the way to fully understanding what is happening in the Caribbean in the lead-up to CWC 2007. It explored some of the major challenges facing the eight (8) host countries as they attempt to put on the greatest Cricket World Cup the world has ever seen. Although the CWC 2007 promises significant socio-cultural and political benefits, the region as a whole will need to find creative solutions to issues related to accommodation, the free movement of people between the islands, customs and immigration, event ticketing and security. Additionally, it is becoming more and more apparent that hosting a successful event depends largely on the support of local communities across the region. Consequently, there needs to be an unprecedented network of information sharing and co-ordination that has largely eluded the region thus far.

This paper can be used as a launching pad for future research. In particular, there is a need to explore mega-event management in small island developing states on a more comprehensive scale, from both a macro and micro perspective. Further research is needed on topics such as the political economy of hosting the event; core-periphery relationships related to the governance in world sport; power relationships between nation states in the Caribbean; the role of the media; the actual costs and benefits of hosting these events; longitudinal surveys of resident perceptions and; community participation strategies.

References

Andranovish, G., Burbank, M., Heying, C., (2001) 'Olympic cities: Lessons learned from mega-event politics', *Journal of Urban Affairs* Vol. 23, Issues 2.

Barbados Nation Newspaper (2004), 'Going for the greatest World Cup 2007', *Barbados Nation Newspaper*, 16 May. Available on: http://windiescricket.com/article [Accessed 15 June 2005].

Burbank, M., Andranovish, G., Heying, C., (2002) 'Mega-events, urban development, and public policy', *Review of Policy Research*, Vol. 19, Issues 3, pp. 179–202.

Campbell, J. (2005) 'World Cup 2007 challenging for Lockerbie', *Sunday Trinidad Express*, 29 May, p. 59.

CaribbeanCricket.com (2004), 'No threat to Guyana WC Stadium'. 29 July. Available on: www.caribbeancricket.com [Accessed on 1 August 2004].

CaribbeanCricket.com (2004), 'B'dos gets WC Finals; J'ca gets W.I.'. Available on: www.caribbeancricket.com [Accessed on 6 April 2005].

Caribbean Tourism Organization (CTO) (2005), 'Cricket World Cup & the Caribbean hotel sector: Preparing to perform', *Caribbean Alliance for Sustainable Tourism*, Vol. 17, No. 1. Available on: http://www.cha-cast.com/Publications.htm [Accessed on 10 May 2005].

Caribbean Tourism Organization (CTO) (2001), *Caribbean Tourism Statistical Report 2000–2001*, CTO, Barbados.

Cozier, T. (2004) 'Caribbean facing crisis over World Cup 2007', *Stabroek News*, 29 January. Available on: http://www.landofsixpeoples.com/gynewsjs.htm [Accessed 12 April 2005].

Davidson, O. (2002) 'WICB to earn hefty sum', *Stabroek News*, 4 August. Available on: http://www.landofsixpeoples.com/gynewsjs.htm [Accessed on 21 May 2005]

Devers, S. (2003) 'Hall bowls bouncer at Regional tourism industry', *Stabroek News*, 8 June. Available on: http://www.landofsixpeoples.com/gynewsjs.htm [Accessed on 10 December 2004].

Emery, P.R. (2002) 'Bidding to host a major sports event: The local organizing committee perspective', *The International Journal of Public Sector Management*, Vol. 15, No. 4, pp. 316–335.

Getz, D. (1997) *Event management and event tourism*. New York: Cognizant Communication Corporation.

Guyana Chronicle (2003a) 'Leading hospitality players look at tourism opportunities in CWC 2007' *Guyana Chronicle*, 23 November. Available on: http://www.landofsixpeoples.com/gynewsjs.htm [Accessed on 10 December 2004].

———— (2003b) 'CWC 2007 is a big responsibility', *Guyana Chronicle*, 3 December. Available on: http://www.landofsixpeoples. com/ gynewsjs.htm [Accessed on 11 December 2004].

———— (2004a) 'PM Anthony urges better distribution of profits', *Guyana Chronicle*, 29 April. Available on: http://www.landofsix peoples.com/ gynewsjs.htm [Accessed on 11 December 2004].

———— (2004b) 'Hosting World Cup Cricket could be tourism watershed', *Guyana Chronicle*, 16 July. Available on: http://www. landofsixpeoples.com/gynewsjs.htm [Accessed on 11 December 2004].

Hall, C.M. (1992) *Hallmark tourist events: Impacts, management and planning*. London: Belhaven Press.

Hines, H. (2004) 'Region could earn $36b from Cricket World Cup', *Jamaica Observer*, 26 July. Available on: http://jamaicaobserver.com {Accessed on 28 July, 2004].

Holder, J. (2003) 'What is at stake for the Caribbean in hosting the Cricket World Cup 2007 event – An address to the CTO Teachers Forum'. Available on: www.onecaribbean.org [Accessed on 23 February 2005].

Hosein, A. (2005) 'Region's hosting of World Cup 2007 … Trouble ahead!', *Trinidad Express Sports*, 14 April, pp. 18–20.

International Cricket Council (ICC) (2005a) 'Senior police representatives arrive from across the region for Cricket World Cup planning meetings', ICC. Available on: www.icc-cricket.com [Accessed on 15 June 2005].

———- (2005b) 'Cricket World Cup calls for a team effort', ICC. Available on: www.icc-cricket.com [Accessed on 10 March 2005].

———— (n.d.) 'ICC CWC 2007 venue summary', ICC. Available on: www.icc-cricket.com [Accessed on 8 April 2005].

John, A. (2004) 'Global games: Culture, political economy and sport in the globalised world of the 21st century', *Third World Quarterly*, Vol. 25, Issue 7: pp. 1325–1337.

Kaieteur News (2004) 'Regional Govts. set up committee for World Cup 2007', *Kaieteur News*, 10 July. Available on: http://www.landofsix peoples.com/gynewsjs.htm [Accessed on 10 March 2005].

Mohammed, F. (2005) 'Wake-up call for Windies World Cup', *Trinidad Express*, 8 July, p. 53.

Pestano, C. (2003) 'Huge economic benefits for hosts of World Cup 2007 matches', *Stabroek News*, 13 June. Available on: http://www. landofsixpeoples.com/news304/ns3112310.htm [Accessed on 10 December 2004].

Reece, T. (2005) 'Ambush marketing…and the World Cup Cricket 2007', *Trinidad Express Business*, 23 March, pp. 13–14.

Spooner, P. (2003) '$40 million Asia hit for Windies', *Guyana Chronicle*, 4 July. Available on: http://www.landofsixpeoples.com/gynewsjs.htm [Accessed on 11 December 2004].

Stabroek News (2002) '2007 World Cup Cricket to test single market – Carrington', *Stabroek News*, 19 July. Available on: http:// www.landofsixpeoples.com/gynewsjs.htm [Accessed on 5 June 2005].

———— (2003) 'Banks urged to help Caribbean businesses benefit from ICC CWC 2007', *Stabroek News*, 4 December. Available on: http:// www.landofsixpeoples.com/gynewsjs.htm [Accessed on 5 June 2005].

———-(2004) 'Regional intelligence network highest priority – CARICOM crime meeting', *Stabroek News*, 6 March. Available on: http://www. landofsixpeoples.com/gynewsjs.htm [Accessed on 5 April 2005].

Street, C. (2005) 'A closer look at World Cup 2007', *Trinidad Express Business*, 27 July, pp. 4-5.

Trinidad Express (2004) 'Caribbean leaders pleased with ICC decision on World Cup venues', *Trinidad Express*, 7 July, p. 76.

Vice, T. (2005) 'Much talk, little action as 2007 World Cup looms', *Trinidad Sunday Express*, 8 May, p. 65.

Waitt, G. (2003) 'Social impacts of the Sydney Olympics', *Annals of Tourism Research*, Vol. 30, No. 1, pp. 194-215.

West Indies Cricket Board (WICB) (2002a) 'World Cup 2007: Business opportunities for the private sector – Part III', WICB, 1 December. Available on: http://windiescricket.com/article [Accessed on 23 November 2004].

———— (2002b) 'World Cup 2007: Business opportunities for the private sector — Part I', WICB, 1 December. Available on: http:// windiescricket.com/article [Accessed on 23 November 2004].

———— (2002c) 'World Cup 2007: Business opportunities for the private sector☐— Part II', WICB, 8 DecemberAvailable on: http://windies cricket.com/article [Accessed on 23 November 2004].

———— (2003a) 'T & T airport expresses regret over Australian gear theft', WICB, 6 June. Available on: http://windiescricket.com/article [Accessed on 30 June 2005].

———— (2003b) 'Barbados confirms Kensington for World Cup Bid', WICB, 4 January. Available on: http://windiescricket.com/article [Accessed on 23 November 2004].

———— (2004a) 'WICB President predicts 2007 will be best ever World Cup', WICB, 6 June. Available on: http://windiescricket.com/article [Accessed on 15 June 2005].

———— (2004b) 'Cricket World Cup Bid opens February 19', WICB, 16 February. Available on: http://windiescricket.com/article [Accessed on 15 June 2005].

———— (2004c) 'ICC World Cup Windies 2007 Bid Books delivered', WICB, 21 February. Available on: http://windiescricket.com/article [Accessed on 15 June 2005].

———— (2004d) 'St. Kitts/Nevis submit letter of intent for 2007 World Cup', WICB, 10 March. Available on: http://windiescricket.com/article [Accessed on 15 June 2005].

———— (2004e) 'Separate groups for Windies, Aussie, Indians, English at 2007 World Cup', WICB, 21 February. Available on: http://windies cricket.com/article [Accessed on 15 June 2005].

———— (2004f) 'Report on 2007 World Cup accommodation, transportation by August', WICB, 30 March. Available on: http://windies cricket.com/article [Accessed on 15 June 2005].

———— 2004g) 'It's Barbados!! ICC World Cup West Indies 2007', WICB. Available on: http://windiescricket.com/article [Accessed on 16 June 2005].

———— (2005a) 'ICC Cricket World Cup West Indies 2007 Inc. to short-list tour, travel & hospitality bidders', WICB, 6 April. Available on: http://windiescricket.com/article [Accessed on 16 June 2005].

———— (2005b) 'ICC Cricket World Cup Official Tour Operator selected', WICB, 21 June. Available on: http://windiescricket.com/article [Accessed on 25 June 2005].

———— (2005c) 'US$100 million insurance coverage for 2007 World Cup', WICB, 7 May. Available on: http://windiescricket.com/article [Accessed on 23 June 2005].

———— (2005d) 'Q and A with Chris Dehring on Venues for ICC Cricket World Cup 2007', WICB, 21 March. Available on: http://windies cricket.com/article [Accessed on 16 June 2005].

Wilkinson, P. F. (1997) *Tourism policy and planning: Case studies from the Commonwealth Caribbean.* New York: Cognizant Communication Corporation, p. 162.

Wilkinson, B. (2004) 'Caribbean governments bail out airline again', *New York Amsterdam News*, Vol. 95, Issue 30, 22 July. Available on: http://web11.epnet.com [Accessed on 3 February 2005].

Williams, C. (2004) 'T&T to spend $140m on World Cup', *Trinidad Express*, 9 July, p. 86.

World Cup St. Lucia (WCSL) (2004) 'The Saint Lucia Bid for Cricket World Cup West Indies — 2007', WCSL. Available on: http://windies cricket.com [Accessed on 10 May 2005].

PLANNING FOR RESORT REGENERATION: THE ROLE OF THE OLYMPIC 2012 BID FOR WEYMOUTH AND PORTLAND, DORSET (UK)

Debbie Sadd and Caroline Jackson

School of Service Management, Bournemouth University (UK)

Introduction

The aim of this paper is to investigate the role of hosting the 2012 Summer Olympic and Paralympic Games for the English seaside resort of Weymouth and neighbouring Isle of Portland, Dorset. This is done through discussing the resort life cycle theories of Butler (1980) and Russell and Faulkner (1998), and investigating where events can 'fit' into these lifecycle theories. Weymouth claims to be 'The First Resort' because King George III and the Royal Family spent their holidays there over 200 years ago (Weymouth and Portland Borough Council, hereinafter WPBC). Like many English resorts Weymouth has suffered a decline in the number of tourism visitors and was therefore awarded the last of the Tourism Development Action Programmes in 1992 to encourage key organisations to think strategically about their planning to overcome the processes of decline (Agarwal, 1999). This was seen not be a success (Agarwal, 2002) and the interest here is whether hosting the Olympics could be the external driver to assist in the regeneration process.

This paper places the hosting of events into the overall tourism planning process and identifies the need to consider positive and negative impacts on the local community i.e. beyond the economic impacts. The Weymouth and Portland National Sailing Academy (hereinafter WPNSA), was built as a centre of excellence for sailing and is now finding itself host to the sailing events of the 2012 Games; the only event wholly held outside of London. This paper was written before the announcement that London had won the bid to host the 2012 Summer

Olympic Games and research undertaken in 2004 when London had been short-listed as a candidate city but were running third in the evaluation stakes. It was also at a time when the Summer Games were at the forefront of people's minds with the Athens Olympics about to be held in August.

Increasingly, towns and cities are using events as a means of serving a host of policy objectives from delivering tourists, to regenerating communities and celebrating moments in time to arousing civic pride, inspiring the arts and stimulating regional economies (Ali-Knight and Robertson, 2004; Bowdin et al., 2001; Derrett, 2003; Hall, 1992). A number of impact studies have been undertaken that identify the different types of impact and conclude that it is difficult to make each factor mutually exclusive and that economic impacts also influence the socio-cultural impacts of the local community (Fredline and Faulkner, 2000; Fredline et al., 2003). Examples have already been seen in Manchester and Cardiff (Law, 1993) where the promotion of sport and leisure events, have contributed to the successful regeneration of city centres and inner areas. A summary of the main reasons for hosting mega-events (Jago and Shaw, 1998) can be found in Table 1.

Resort regeneration

Most mega and major events are hosted in large cities and towns and most research has focused on urban regeneration. This paper focuses on the role of a mega-event on a seaside resort. The history of the 'English Resort' began in the eighteenth and nineteenth century when changes in society such as the increase in leisure time and more disposable income, coupled with transport developments, allowed the populous to visit the seaside. This growth continued until the 1970s and the advent of package holidays overseas. However, it was the inability to change and evolve that led to many resorts failing to provide a product that meets modern expectations and requirements in the quality of entertainment, accommodation and service delivery (Moore, 2001). Resort regeneration, the development of initiatives to prevent economic decline especially seen in UK coastal resorts (Agarwal, 2002), is often linked to resort lifecycles through the theories of Butler (1980), Russell and Faulkner (1998) and Prideaux (2000).

Table 1 Reasons for growth in Mega-Events

1   Positive imaging — putting the region, city and community on the map
    (Monclus, 2003) — Barcelona, (Stamakis et al, 2003), (Law, 1993),
    (Chalkley and Essex, 1999), (Auld and McArthur, 2003)

2   One city seeks to emulate the success of another city
    (Madden, 2002), (Searle, 2002), (Toohey and Veal, 2001), (Waitt, 2001),
    (Brissenden, 1987)

3   Economic development potential as seen by government
    (Hall, 1992), (Auld and McArthur, 2003), (Jeong, 1999) (Hughes,
    1993), (Crompton &McKay, 1997) (Mathieson and Wall, 1982),

4   Segmentation and specialisation within the tourism market
    (Chalip L, 2002), (Crompton and McKay, 1997),(Morse, 2001),
    (Shackkley, 2000)

5   Availability of government grants for sports, art and culture
    (Hall, 1992), (Gunn, 1994), Persson, 2002)

6   Attracting of investment by the use of profile and image
    (Burgan and Mules, 1992), (Shone and Parry, 2001), (WTO, 1997)

7   Promotion of civic pride and the desire to overcome adverse circum-
    stances
    (Brissenden, 1987), (Chalkley and Essex, 1999), (Law, 1993)

8   The changing nature of leisure activity in western society
    (Boniface and Cooper, 1994),(Cooper and Fletcher, 2000),(Faulkner et
    al, 2000), (Pearce and Butler, 1999), (Crompton and McKay, 1997)

Source: Sadd 2004 (adapted from Hall, 1992; Getz, 1997)

Whilst destinations can have life-cycles (Butler, 1980; Faulkner et al., 2000), an examination of Butlers' resort cycle model (Figure 1) highlights the need to ensure that the organisation of events should be directly linked to an overall resort development strategy. This is because many events, whilst taking place in tourist areas, are not just dependent on the tourist market for their success or even organised specifically for tourists. Most events will attract local residents and tourists or be organised by community groups for their own purposes. Getz (1991), questions Butler's theory by arguing that some destinations are constantly evolving thereby concurring with the Russell and Faulkner model (Figure 2). Events have been used to add differentiation to the product, lengthen stay and encourage repeat business such as the Edinburgh

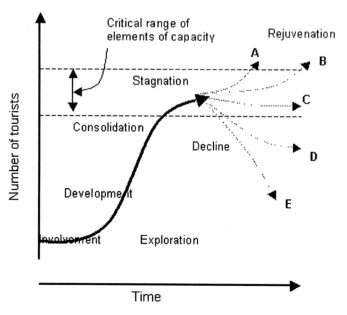

Figure 1   **Butler's Model (1980) adapted to illustrate the role and timing of the introduction of events**

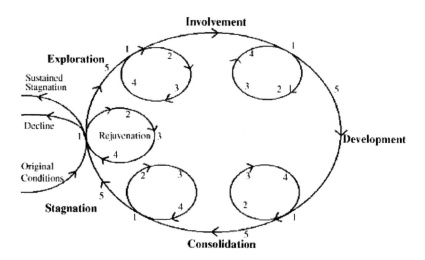

Figure 2   **Russell and Faulkner's cyclical representation of Butler's lifecycle model with entrepreneurial triggers**

Festival (Ali-Knight and Robertson, 2004). In English seaside resorts the overall lifecycle does not reflect the annual seasonal life-cycle created by the influx of tourists during the school summer holidays.

Russell and Faulkner (1998) believe that 'triggering' mechanisms cause sub-cycles to occur within each stage of the model so that the life-cycle is not linear but constantly evolving and re-inventing itself. Events can play this role within resort destinations through their uniqueness and experience. Events are used to reduce the extremes in seasonality of a seaside resort with the development of facilities and then programmes to cater for target markets such as the conference market during the shoulder months of the tourism season. This concept could be broadened to use major and mega events as part of the broader resort strategic development and the resort lifecycle used to help identify when these 'entrepreneurial' triggers should be used to continue the cycle of development.

Russell and Faulkner (1998) argue that as these demands change, it is the 'entrepreneurial' drive and activity that brings the destination back into the Butler's Lifecycle model and therefore drives the destination forward.

Agarwal (2002) discusses the resort restructuring opportunities through analysis of the resort lifecycle and included Weymouth within her case studies. She writes that whilst Butler's model is extended to include regeneration as an option, little is known about the role regeneration can play and how restructuring is achieved. Events in seaside resorts have predominantly focused on conferences, entertainment and currently casinos as catalysts for regeneration. Resorts have found it difficult to diversify from the sand and sun that was their attraction pre-1970 and have therefore found it hard to compete with overseas resorts. Although part of the 'package' few English resorts have used sport or sports events as a main attraction (Eastbourne successfully hosts the Lawn Tennis Association's Women's International Championships that acts as a warm-up event for Wimbledon). Cowes has become synonymous with the hallmark sailing regatta but is really a seaport town and not a seaside resort (that has a beach as a main attraction). It will be interesting to see if Weymouth and Portland, as a satellite centre, will benefit from the London 2012 Games. Research undertaken on Garfield County, a community area close to Salt Lake City Winter Olympics 2002, were indifferent to the Games but supported the idea of a marketing awareness campaign throughout the Games (Deccio and Baloglu, 2002). Weymouth and Portland residents won't be peripheral to the sailing events but will be from the main centre of action in London.

Tourism planning and associated impacts

Tourism planning and resort planning in particular, with the three levels suggested by Gunn (1994), national, regional strategic and local, need to be integrated to produce an adoptable strategic vision. Weymouth and Portland unsuccessfully tried to utilise the Tourism Development Action Plan to regenerate itself (1992–95), and now they await the opportunity to host an Olympic event to be more successful in this area. Turco et al. (2002) argue that the planning of events should take a holistic approach, looking beyond the economic impacts, gather information regarding the communities and special interest groups and if used effectively may help to develop good community relations, thereby overcoming objections and limiting the possible negative impacts. Furthermore, events should play a role in the destination tourism plan and that sound planning should accompany the pursuit of events. (Andersson, 1999; Getz, 1997). The Appendix demonstrates strategies aimed at communities and destinations contemplating a bid for a mega event or in the process of planning an event.

Place distinctiveness of Weymouth and Portland

Agarwal (2002) believes it important to recognise and appreciate a resort's place distinctiveness and then to use this in the restructuring strategies to offset the possible decline. In Weymouth and Portland's case, the local distinctiveness is its unique sailing waters and the decision to support the building of man-made features to complement and capitalise on the distinctiveness of not only the harbour, but also the adjacent setting of the World Heritage Coastline. These attributes were recognised by Lord Coe and Princess Royal, at the official opening ceremony of the WPNSA in June, 2005 (WPNSA).

Weymouth is a medium sized seaside resort on the south coast of England, 160 miles from London, with a population of approximately 60,000. It has sandy beaches and shallow offshore waters with a sheltered harbour containing reputably some of the best sailing waters in the world. The resort traditionally has been a family destination attracting a strong domestic tourist market base but has suffered in the last 30 years due to the increase in overseas travel (Argarwal, 1999, 2002). Weymouth is connected to the Isle of Portland which is the former home of the Royal Navy Base, HMS Osprey, and it is upon this land that the South West Regional Development Agency (SWRDA) have developed the Weymouth and Portland National Sailing Academy (WPNSA) with assistance from the Royal Yachting Association (RYA), Dorset County Council, Weymouth and Portland Borough Council, Sport England, English Institute of Sport and other sponsors.

The Weymouth and Portland National Sailing Academy

It is this venue that will host the 2012 sailing events for both the main summer Olympic and Paralympic Games. The WPNSA was formed in 1999 as a not-for-profit organisation to acquire the lease on the site, to bid for funds and grants and to facilitate the building of the centre and yet also to work alongside the London 2012 bid team. A local company, Sail Force Ltd, won the tender to run the centre with the overall responsibility of the entire operation remaining with the WPNSA. Whether this set up will continue to be successful without any conflict prior to the hosting of the 2012 sailing will remain to be seen. The original three aims of the WPNSA were to promote the sport of sailing, provide community use of the facilities and to contribute to substantial local economic regeneration (WPNSA).

For Weymouth and Portland, the sailing facilities have been developed irrespective of the Olympic bid as the intention was to build 'state of the art' new facilities for sailing that were more accessible than Cowes on the Isle of Wight. This uniqueness is in itself a catalyst for change because of the ability of the centre to host elite sailing events. The additional facilities that will be required to host the Olympic and Paralympic sailing events will cost an estimated £17 million. It is planned to utilise and develop existing accommodation stocks but also to use cruise liners to accommodate the visiting VIP's, officials, media and competitors. Additional pontoons will be required so it is planned to build a new marina that will be sold off after the Games and to build temporary structures for the duration of the Games. Spectators will be encouraged to use park and ride facilities to reach the open air viewing areas to be positioned around the perimeter of the harbour and bay (Sadd, 2004).

The WPNSA is already playing its part in hosting major events, including the J24 World Championships in September 2005; the Volvo Youth Sailing ISAF World Championships, the 29er World Championships and the 49er European Championships in July 2006. The main impacts identified by the Borough Council for these events are economic, media coverage and the lasting legacy of demonstrating an international 'Weymouth welcome'. They also develop event management abilities in the operation of the event and demonstrate how the local infrastructure, facilities, services and organisations are able to coordinate a successful world class event (WPBC, 2005).

Primary research

Research was carried out in Weymouth and Portland as soon as the announcement was made in 2002 of the UK bid for the 2012 Olympic Games. One of the aims was to identify the relevance and importance of the bidding and hosting of the Games for the local community. Quantitative and qualitative research was undertaken with key stakeholders and the residents of the Borough. The role of the latter in the planning for the hosting of events in general and the sailing as part of the Olympics was an important part of this research. The research undertook to investigate both the positive and potentially negative impacts of hosting events. How relevant were the characteristics of Doxey's irritant factors in this case?

The research to evaluate the community's views on the impacts of hosting events within Weymouth and Portland was carried out with the assistance of the Borough Council, Local Chamber of Commerce, Sailing Authorities, Citizen's Panel and individual citizens via questionnaires (447 returned from 1000 with 27 spoiled) with follow-up semi-structured interviews. The respondents recognised the significance of hosting festivals and events not only as generators of income, but also as civic celebrations. The relative importance of events to the lives and community of the residents of Weymouth and Portland generated a 42% response rate for the questionnaire. The positive and negative impacts identified go beyond only the economic and reach into the lives of the residents and the image they have of themselves and their community.

Despite the presence in Weymouth of the Citizen's Panel, the Community Partnership and the council newsletter, the majority of residents, as evidenced within the questionnaire responses, do not feel involved in the decisions their council makes. The Citizen's Panel is heavily weighted towards the 55+ age bracket and retired residents portraying a bias that is acknowledged in the research. In addition, it was felt by some residents that the business community and some members in particular, have a much louder say in the activities that take place in Weymouth and Portland. Whilst the residents will welcome the sailing events to the area, there is some fear that people, including locals, will stay away from the events due to overcrowding. This displacement has been the subject of research related to the previous Summer and Winter Olympic Games (Hiller, 1998).

The use of events in place distinctiveness

From the community's point of view, it is not the individual life cycles that are of importance, rather the overall portfolio that is of greater importance (Getz, 2000) and in Weymouth and Portland's case their unique ability to be able to host events relating to the sea and military connections. Weymouth markets itself as the "eventful" resort and believing itself to have a "level of expertise" in organising military parades in addition to their record of hosting Tall Ships on an unprecedented three occasions. Within the research carried out in 2004, the overwhelming positive impacts of events on the community were evidenced by 58% of the questionnaire respondents indicating a desire for more large-scale events to be held in the town with many indicating the preference for more nautical events as seen in Figures 3 and 4.

Weymouth and Portland community issues and involvement

Any event associated with the Olympics, is expected to generate large external benefits where the benefits are widely spread and justify funding from public monies. Getz (2003) argues that events can be categorised by the strain the event places on the destination's

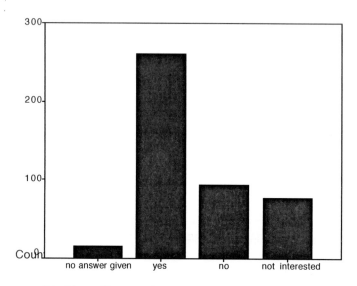

Would you like more large scale events in Weymouth?

Figure 3   Capacity for residents to accept more tourists

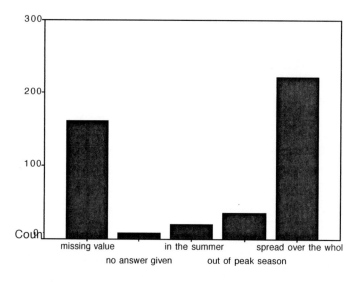

when would you like to see more tourists?

Figure 4   Public interest in large-scale events in the areas

infrastructure and whilst communities may not need new facilities, they encourage the event as a catalyst for positive infrastructure improvements because external funds can be obtained. For many residents of Weymouth and Portland, the issue of the relief road is of vital importance to the impacts of any major events within the surrounding area. As the London 2012 bid was successful, there is added impetus for the scheme to get the approval needed to progress within the short term, otherwise the road will continue to be a contentious issue for the town's residents and a source of confrontation with the council.

Without the Olympics bid being successful, it was anticipated that the road issue would not be resolved quickly and the whole area, including the economic well being of the town, would suffer greatly as more businesses relocated due to the road congestion (interviews with residents, 2004). They have already lost the distribution centre for New Look, a locally based national retail clothing business. However, this raises the issue of how events are used to get through changes that are not acceptable to all. What was quite a powerful environmental lobby against the relief road may now be sidestepped for the necessity of the road to carry the capacity required of the Olympic and Paralympic sailing events.

Doxey's often quoted irritant index includes congestion as a factor causing dissatisfaction amongst local residents (Cooper et al., 2005; Shaw and Williams, 2000). This can be caused by people or by their use of transport, especially cars. There will be cases of "The Los Angeles" effect (Hall, 1992, and Getz, 1991), where the local residents will go out of town for the duration of the event to avoid the negative impacts caused by the road congestion. Some visitors may even stay away, who would normally visit the area, due to over inflated prices, perceived or real, during the period of the Olympic events as seen in Athens 2004 (Carlin, 2003).

Carrying capacity issues

One of the issues identified by the research was that of visitor numbers. Carrying capacity relates to the point beyond which further levels of visitation or development would lead to unacceptable deterioration in the physical environment, the visitors' enjoyment and residents' acceptance (O'Reilly, 1986; Theobald, 1999). Carrying capacity plays a pivotal role by intervening in the relationship between visitor and resources. The character of the resource — i.e. its natural features — is equally important and the resort/area must decide its physical limits and robustness to continued tourism development (Mathieson and Wall, 1982; O'Reilly, 1986).

For sports events there are two types of visitors: participants and spectators. Different types of events focus on one or the other (Green, 2001) or lie on a continuum from being competitor to spectator driven (Gratton, Dobson and Shibli, 2000). Most sailing events are predominantly participant based but in the case of the Olympic sailing events the host destination will be concerned with both participants and spectators. The London 2012 bid document estimated attendance of 15,000 per day, yet the local council estimate the figure to be far higher and even in excess of 70,000 per day. This is within the town's carrying capacity as evidenced through their hosting of the Tall Ships Festival on three separate occasions when the town accommodated over 100,000 visitors. In this instance it is easier to estimate the number of participants, and there are estimated to be 400 sailors from 61 nations competing for 54 medals in 126 races (WPBC).

Weymouth and Portland's forward planning

One conclusion derived from the research, via the literature review and interviews, is that each event is unique and that whilst there are trends that can be seen to occur, the key to success lies in forward planning. Weymouth and Portland Council began planning as soon as it was announced that the UK were preparing a bid for the 2012 Olympic Games, although the WPNSA was planned before this, but it is only in the last 12 months that the community has become more involved. Athens did not plan early enough and suffered from adverse publicity, culminating in many potential visitors staying away and some events being left undersold. Conversely, the organisers of the Beijing Games have been told to slow down as many facilities are already near completion, and will need to be 'mothballed' for three years, whilst not generating any income.

In Weymouth and Portland the local community have also been involved in forward planning with school children designing posters and leaflets illustrating the natural features of the area. Local businesses are carrying large banners on the outside of their buildings supporting the 2012 bid and advertising the important role Weymouth and Portland are to play if the bid is successful. Local College students made a DVD for the International Olympic Committee to see the benefits of hosting the sailing in the Weymouth and Portland area.

Opportunities for regeneration

The opportunities for the Weymouth and Portland area to regenerate are already recognised through the research questionnaire by the residents and several suggestions have been put forward for ways to do this irrespective of the Olympic sailing coming to the area, including the upgrading of seaside accommodation owned by the council into 'boutique' style hotels to attract wealthier visitors to the area. Even if the result of the Singapore IOC vote had not been in favour of a London 2012 Games, the WPNSA still intended to hold world class sailing events, although the opportunities for resort regeneration may not have been as immediate. The fact that several world class sailors and windsurfers have relocated to live in the Weymouth and Portland area because of the natural facilities, in addition to the WPNSA, may yet encourage more people to move to the area and thus regenerate the towns image through its water sports facilities.

Weymouth and Portland Borough Council are very committed to the hosting of the sailing events and they are realistic enough to realise the momentum that has been gained by the bid procedure even on the local population, should continue in its bid to revitalise the image of the town. They are presently redesigning their marketing campaign to include the proximity of the World Heritage coastline, the development of the WPNSA and surrounding areas and in particular the natural facilities of the harbour and beaches. They recognise the economic significance of tourism to the town and are within their tourism team planning events throughout the whole summer to keep the community spirit alive. Press coverage and media interest shown in the area since the July decision has already resulted in several initiatives including the opportunities to advertise the Olympic venue status of the town at every opportunity not just by the council but local businesses and the community at large (Gallivan interview, 2005).

It can be concluded from the research that too much emphasis on the economic benefits should not over shadow the other possible impacts both positive and negative. Whilst the local communities will experience short-term disruption through traffic restrictions, tow-away zones, road closures and car parks converted to other uses (Sadd, 2004); there will be the opportunities for long-term gains especially from resort regeneration through media exposure, community spirit and a relief road. The main strategies and actions that Weymouth and Portland could take are summarised in Table 2.

Table 2   Strategies for Weymouth and Portland to optimise the tourism impacts of 2012

Plan for the long-term

    Regional Development Agency driving development of former Navy Base HMS Osprey. Weymouth and Portland needs to decide where it intends to position itself. Present strategy is to appeal to all sectors of the market but dot hey have the facilities to satisfy these demands with their present resources and infrastructure. Possibility of upgrading accommodation and extending tourism into shoulder seasons through the use of events.

Optimise facility development and use of existing facilities

    Weymouth and Portland in conjunction with the Weymouth and Portland National Sailing Academy (WPSNA) and the 2012 organising committee have recognised that oversupply of facilities could be detrimental in the long run. Other than the on-going developments at the WPSNA and significance of the development of the relief road, the additional accommodation and catering requirements are all too be temporary arrangements for the duration of the Games. The additional facilities required at the WPSNA include further mooring, which will post the Games be sold off as a private marina. Actively market proximity to World Heritage Coastline, especially the Jurassic Coastline.

Plan for sustained awareness and image-making efforts

    Combat negative publicity, as seen in the British Press and their criticisms of the London 2012 bid (Woodridge, 2004, *Daily Mail*, May 22nd). Involve the press from the planning and feasibility stages right through to the after event summaries and looking to the future. Already the council are working closely with the 2012 team with press releases and in addition the council are keeping the residents up to date with developments via the local press, council website and the chamber of trade.

Tourist facilitation

    Overcome resident objections which are mainly based around traffic congestion. The relief road issue will overcome most of this. Any evidence of Doxey's Index of Irritation must be handled by the

Table 2 (cont.)

organisers in Weymouth and Portland and must consider the needs of the local population.

Target marketing

The opportunity presents itself for the council to develop 'top end' accommodation within its seafront property portfolio to satisfy the demands of more discerning visitors which may in turn present the opportunity to upgrade its other facilities to satisfy their demands.

The 'Towards 2015' tourism drive of South-West Tourism talks about quality over quantity and this initiative would satisfy this drive (Sadd, 2005).

Combat displacement effects

Get the locals involved as volunteers despite the fact that the events are taking place 160 miles away from the main Olympic site. Let them feel involved in what is taking place in their town. Residents must be persuaded that the event is so unique that they should forego their other trips. Council to manage the licensing of products and concessions to try and avoid temporary price inflations.

Dispersal of benefits

The very nature of the events taking place around the harbour will allow for management of the visitors. A park and ride scheme will help traffic control. The local emergency services already have their blueprint in place.

Maximising tourism benefits

Spread the events beyond the August/September key months and in the years leading up to 2012. Already the WPSNA are hosting world class sailing events and should encourage the community to support these events and help where possible. Hold more community events at the WPSNA where possible and invite the community to sail. This in turn will encourage more tourists to visit the area, especially those with an interest in watersports.

Future legacy of the WPNSA

John Tweed, Director of Development at the WPNSA, believes that the centre will provide affordable, accessible and socially inclusive community facilities to allow local people to be introduced to sailing and water sports and to progress through all levels. The Royal Yachting Association charity, Sailability, is fully engaged to ensure leisure and competitive requirements for disabled people are accommodated in the new academy. Tweed further believes that the profile of not just

Weymouth and Portland but the region as a whole will be enhanced through the building of the new centre irrespective of the 2012 bid's success through the employment of 150 full-time equivalent jobs and the resulting £5.9 million increase in demand for local businesses.

The publicity being generated for the academy and the area through the bid process is helping to establish the centre and the area as a World Class sailing and water sports venue. The opportunity to focus worldwide television audiences on the area will be immense, especially within the UK because of the success of Team GB at the Athens Olympic Games. The media exposure opportunities are considerable, especially through major sailing events as identified earlier. Media coverage will be important to encourage the non-sailing community's interest and to overcome any objections to sailing becoming an elitist sport and in particular the WPNSA being for top class sailors. The council's PR representative already describes Weymouth and Portland as an 'eventful resort' thus emphasising the role events play within the Tourism profile of the town. Lord Coe has described the sailing facilities at the WPNSA as the "jewel in the crown" of the UK bid of which Weymouth and Portland are undoubtedly very proud. They plan to keep the momentum going by deciding where they want to be and believing in it.

Conclusion

The opportunities arising from the hosting of events to 'regenerate', as per Butler's lifecycle, must not be assumed to be the universal remedy for areas in decline. A study of the work of Russell and Faulkner (1998) represents a better model for using events within resort regeneration. Whilst events, and even it can be argued the opportunity to bid for major events, can create awareness, raise community spirit and lead to infrastructure improvements, it is the joint co-operation and working together of a multi-agency partnership that will ensure that the event role within any regeneration strategy can be successful not just in the short term, but also in the medium and long term as well. This was one of the conclusions reached after the evaluation of the Tourism Development Action Plan (Agarwal, 1999 and 2002). It is hoped that lessons have been learnt from this and that the Olympics will act as a greater external catalyst to change and co-operation than the £300,000 three year TDAP funding.

Weymouth and Portland Borough Council recognises its distinctiveness and should build upon the momentum of hosting major sailing events to expand its tourism market to the "shoulder" months, thereby nor relying solely upon its summer trade. The Olympic sailing events do not necessarily help with this because the races will be held between 27 July to 12 August for the Olympics and 29 August to 9 September 2012 for the Paralympics. The opportunities present themselves with the development of the sporting facilities at the WPNSA coupled with the natural facilities of the harbour and surrounding waters, thus satisfying the entrepreneurial 'triggers' referred to by Russell and Faulkner (1998). The community issues including the relief road developments if addressed satisfactorily would have overcome any local objections to the hosting of the Games and encourage community involvement in the regeneration of the town (NB this is now not likely to occur).

In terms of the resort restructuring literature (Agarwal, 2002; Morgan, 1994), Weymouth is diversifying its product portfolio from relying on the summer beach to special events and the Jurassic Coast. Agarwal (2002) however identifies that other resorts are also diversifying their attractions to include events, historic and maritime resources. What will give Weymouth and Portland their uniqueness and distinguish them from other resorts is by developing a specialisation in sailing events. This is something that is based on a natural resource and enhanced by built facilities like the WPNSA. No other resort is going to be able to copy this. Through the Olympic and Paralympic sailing events Weymouth will be on the world media stage and is competing globally for international sailing events. No other tourism development could achieve this potential step change. However, Weymouth and Portland are not London and will need to work together as a community with LOCOG to maximise the leverage potential that the Games can afford them and beyond.

References

Ali-Knight, J. and Robertson, M. (2004) 'Introduction to arts, culture and leisure', in I. Yeoman, et al. (eds) *Festival and events management*. Oxford: Elsevier Butterworth-Heinemann.

Andersson, T. D. Persson, C. Sahlberg, B. and Strom, L-I. (1999) *The impact of mega-events*. Ostersund, Sweden: European Tourism Research Institute.

Agarwal, S. (1999) 'Restructuring and local economic development: implications for seaside resort regeneration in Southwest Britain', *Tourism Management* Vol. 20: pp. 511–522.

Agarwal, S. (2002) 'Restructuring seaside tourism: the resort lifecycle', *Annals of Tourism Research* Vol. 29, No.1: pp. 25–55.

Auld, T. and McArthur, S. (2003) 'Does event-driven tourism provide economic benefits? A case study from the Manawatu region of New Zealand', *Tourism Economics* Vol.9, No. 2: pp.191–201.

Boniface, B.G. and Cooper, C.P. (1994) *The geography of travel and tourism.* London: Heinemann.

Bowdin, G. McDonnell, I. Allen, J. and O'Toole, W. (2001) *Event management.* Oxford: Butterworth-Heinemann.

Burgan, B. and Mules, T. (1992) 'Economic impact of sporting events', *Annals of Tourism Research* Vol.19: pp. 700–710.

Butler, R.W. (1980) 'The concept of a tourist area cycle of evolution implications for management of resources', *Canadian Geographer* Vol. 24: pp. 5–12.

Carlin, G. (2003) 'City and sport marketing strategy: the case of Athens 2004,' *The Sports Journal* Vol. 6, No. 2.

Chalkley, B. and Essex, S. (1999) 'Urban Development through hosting international events: a history of the Olympic games', *Planning Perspectives* Vol. 14: pp. 369–394.

Cooper, C. Fletcher, J. Fyall, A. Gilbert, D. Wanhill, S. (2005) *Tourism, principles and practice (3rd edition).* Harlow: Longman.

Crompton, J. L. and McKay, S. L. (1997) 'Motives of visitors attending festival events', *Annals of Tourism Research* Vol. 24, No.2: pp. 425–439.

Deccio, C. and Baloglu, S. (2002) 'Nonhost Community Resident Reactions to the 2002 Winter Olympics: The Spillover Impacts,' *Journal of Travel Research* Vol. 41: pp. 46–56.

Derrett, R. (2000) 'Making sense of how festivals demonstrate a community's sense of place', *Event Management* Vol. 8: pp. 49–58.

Faulkner, B. Moscardo, G. and Laws, E. (eds) (2000) *Tourism in the 21st Century.* London: Continuum.

Fredline, E. and Faulkner, B. (2000) 'Community perceptions of the impacts of events' in *Events Beyond 2000*, Australian Centre for Event Management.

Fredline, L., Jago, L. and Deery, M. (2003) 'The development of a generic scale to measure the social impacts of events,' *Event Management* Vol. 8: pp. 23–37.

Getz, D. (1991) *Festivals, special events and tourism.* New York: Van Nostrand Reinhold.

—— (1997) *Event management and event tourism.* New York: Cognizant Communication Corporation.

—— (2000) 'Festivals and Special Events: Life Cycle and Saturation Issues', in W. C. Gartner and D. W. Lime (eds). *Trends in outdoor leisure and tourism.* CABI.

—— (2003) 'Sport Event Tourism: planning, development and marketing', in S. Hudson (ed) *Sport and adventure tourism.* New York: Haworth Hospitality Press.

Gisborne, J. (2005) J24 World Championship event information sheet, unpublished, Weymouth and Portland Borough Council.

Gratton, C., Dobson, N. and Shibli, S. (2000) 'The economic importance of major sports events: a case study of six events'. *Managing Leisure* Vol. 5: pp. 17–28.

Green, B. C. (2001) 'Leveraging subculture and identity to promote sport events,' *Sport Management Review* Vol. 4: pp. 1–19.

Gunn, C. (1994) *Tourism planning.* USA: Taylor and Francis.

Hall, C. M. (1992) *Hallmark tourist events: impacts, management and planning.* London: Belhaven Press.

Hall, C. M. (1994) *Tourism and politics: policy, power and place* Chichester: Wiley.

Hiller, H. H. (1998) 'Assessing the impact of mega-events: a linkage model', *Current Issues in Tourism* Vol. 1. No. 1: pp. 47–57.

Hughes, H. L. (1993) 'Olympic tourism and urban regeneration', *Festival and Event Tourism* Vol.1: pp.157–162.

Jago, L. and Shaw, R. (1998) 'Special events: a conceptual and differential framework,' *Festival Management and Event Tourism* Vol. 5, No. 1/ 2: pp. 21–32.

Jeong, G-H. (1999) 'Tourism mega-events,' *Annals of Tourism Research* Vol.15, No. 2: pp. 272–273.

Law, C. M. (1993) *Urban Tourism: attracting visitors to large cities.* London: Mansell.

Madden, J. (2002) 'The economic consequences of the Sydney Olympics: the CREA/Arthur study,' *Current Issues in Tourism* Vol. 5, No. 1: pp. 7–21.

Mathieson, A. and Wall, G. (1982) *Tourism: economic, physical and social impacts.* Harlow: Longman.

Monclus, F. J. (2003) 'The Barcelona Model: an original formula? From reconstruction to strategic urban projects,' *Planning Perspectives* Vol.18: pp. 399–421.

Morgan, M. (1994) 'Homogeneous products: the future of established resorts' in W. Theobald (ed) *Global tourism: the next decade.* Oxford: Butterworth-Heinemann, pp. 378–395.

Moore, P. (2001) 'Turning the tide,' *Locum Destination review* pp. 54–56.

Morse, J. (2001) 'The Sydney 2000 Olympic Games: how the Australian Tourist Commission leveraged the games for tourism,' *Journal of Vacation Marketing* Vol.7, No. 2: pp. 101–107.

O'Reilly, O. M. (1986) 'Tourism carrying capacity: concepts and issues,' *Tourism Management* Vol. 7, No. 4: pp. 254–258.

Pearce, D. G. and Butler, R. W. (eds) (1999) *Contemporary issues in tourism development.* London: Routledge.

Persson, C. (2002) 'The Olympic Site Decision,' *Tourism Management* Vol.23: pp.27–36.

Prideaux, B. (2000) 'The resort development spectrum: a new approach to modelling resort development,' *Tourism Management* Vol. 21: pp. 225–240.

Ritchie, J. R. B. (1984) 'Assessing the impacts of hallmark events: conceptual and research issues,' *Journal of Travel Research* Vol. 23, No. 1: pp. 2–11.

Russell, R. and Faulkner, B. (1998) 'Reliving the destination lifecycle in Coolangetta. An historical perspective on the rise, decline and rejuvenation of an Australian seaside resort', in E. Laws, B. Faulkner and G. Moscardo (eds) *Embracing and managing change in tourism: International case studies.* London: Routledge.

Sadd, D. J. (2004) The impacts of mega-events at satellite venues: case study of Weymouth and Portland as a possible Olympic Sailing Venue. Unpublished Masters dissertation, Bournemouth University.

Searle, G. (2002) 'Uncertain legacy: Sydney's Olympic stadiums,' *European Planning Studies* Vol. 10, No. 7: pp.846–860.

Shaw, G. and Williams, A. M. (2000) *Critical issues in tourism: a geographical perspective (2nd Edition).* Oxford: Blackwell.

Shone, A. and Parry, B. (2004) *Successful event management: a practical handbook. 2nd edition.* London: Thomson.

Stamakis, H. Gargalianos, D. Afthinos, Y and Nassis, P. (2003) 'Venue contingency planning for the Sydney 2000 Olympic games,' *Facilities* Vol. 21, No. 5/6: pp.115–125.

Theobald, W. F. (1998) *Global tourism* Oxford: Butterworth-Heinemann.

Toohey, K. and Veal, A. J. (2001) *The Olympic Games* Wallingford: CABI.

Turco, D. M. Riley, R. and Swart, K. (2002) *Sport tourism.* Morgantown, WV: Fitness Information Technology Inc.

Waitt, G. (2001) 'Social Impacts of the Sydney Olympics', *Annals of Travel Research* Vol. 30, No. 1: pp. 194–215.

Weymouth and Portland Borough Council (WPBC) www.weymouth.gov.uk

Weymouth and Portland National Sailing Academy (WPNSA) www.wpnsa.org.uk

Appendix

Generic Strategies for optimising the tourism impacts of mega-events

Plan for the long-term

Specifically plan for pre and post event impacts as well as the event itself. Have a clear vision for the future and focus on the intended legacies of the event. Clear guidelines and responsibilities of organisers and reporting channels by planning the organisational and marketing evolution necessary to ensure long-term benefits for all.

Optimise facility development and use of existing facilities

The development of new facilities represents one of the largest costs and entails great risks of over –supply with limited use after the event. The use of cruise ships to supply temporary accommodation where feasible is a popular option as is turning accommodation facilities into low cost affordable housing or university accommodation as seen in Atlanta (Toohey and Veal, 2001)

Plan for sustained awareness and image-making efforts

Smith (1986, in Getz, 1991, p.253) notes, "it is the media, backed by word-of-mouth which generates and controls the hype". Getz (1991) also writes that although travel and sports writers have their own specialised readership, it is news reporters who have the largest audiences and therefore the biggest influence. In return the television distribution rights for the coverage of the Olympics will cost US$800 million for the 2006 winter Games and US$1700 million for the 2008 summer Games (Persson, 2002)

Tourist facilitation

Making the stay of the visitors as comfortable as possible. The ease of purchasing tickets must be considered on a global scale with the utmost precision to combat "black market" being sold at inflated prices. Similarly, the ease of entry for all nationals across international borders must be considered and the provision of information in as many languages as possible. The host population must be willing and helpful to all visitors.

Target marketing

The possibility of attracting higher-yield, quality visitors must be considered as opposed to the mass market, large volumes. Residents however, should not be excluded

Combat displacement effects

In order to avoid visitors staying away through fear of overcrowding, price inflations, crime and terrorism, a concentrated programme of information and an image-making campaign must be initiated as soon as possible.

Dispersal of benefits

If possible spread the events over a large area to avoid congestion. However, depending on the event it may be more prudent to concentrate facilities to reduce costs and to make it a more pleasant experience for the visitor.

Maximising tourism benefits

Encourage visitors to stay longer by organising pre and post event celebrations. Use high quality souvenirs to encourage visitors to buy more items and use local suppliers to increase the multiplier effect. Include in the event planning entertainment opportunities, yet do not over-supply permanent facilities.

Sources: Sadd (2004) adapted from Andersson *et al.* (1999)

"EVENTS, DEAR BOY. EVENTS…." CHANCE, OPPORTUNISM AND UNPREDICTABILITY IN PRE-EVENT PLANNING FOR POST-EVENT FUNCTION: A CASE STUDY OF THE BOLTON ARENA.

Phil Binks and Bob Snape

**Department of Sport, Leisure & Tourism Management,
University of Bolton (UK)**

Introduction

The paper on which this article is based was delivered two hours after the announcement of London's success in winning the bid to host the Olympic Games in 2012. On the following day the national newspapers reflected a wave of public enthusiasm for the games and analysed their intended impacts in detail, particularly those involving the construction of venues and their post-Games community legacy. However, in the midst of the celebrations, a minority discordant voice urged recall of past projects in the development of large-scale event-related venues such as Pickett's Lock, the Millennium Dome and Wembley Stadium (*Independent*, 2005). Having earned infamy through their inability to realise the vision of their progenitors these projects had come to serve as a metaphor for an unholy convergence of political, economic and personal ambition and the inherent difficulty of harnessing the optimism generated through the possibility of a sport mega-event to the *realpolitik* of business and complex partnership arrangements. Such partnerships have typically included public, private and voluntary agencies and have become a dominant feature in the building of large scale sport facilities despite evidence to suggest that partnerships in general involve a significant element of risk (Bonney, 2004; McFee, 2002) and that leisure and sport partnerships in particular may not always realise their intended public benefit (Roberts, 2004: pp. 117–120).

65

Events, facilities and communities

The nature of the relationship between events and the venues referred to above is reasonably transparent as major sport events, both national and international, require large stadia for spectator accommodation and, for the largest events such as a football World Cup or an Olympiad, a prestigious venue is a prerequisite for selection as host nation. The cost of hosting such events, including those of constructing the venues, requires a long-term strategic justification in both economic and social terms. However, cost benefit analysis of such events remains a challenging task, particularly as social and environmental impacts do not easily accommodate quantitative analysis (Bramwell, 1997a; Kronthaler and Franz, 2003). Despite the inherent uncertainty and risk in hosting major events, their allure remains strong because, as with Tokyo and Seoul, they heighten the international profile of the host city (Prince, 2005) and because, as is clearly illustrated in the pre-event reception of the London 2012 Olympics, they are seen to provide a platform for economic investment and social benefit (Prystay and Pringle, 2005). Beyond capital cities, events not only retain their capacity to enhance the profile of their host but serve as a signification of provincial and regional renewal as variously exemplified in the European City of Culture award, the Hay Literature Festival and the Commonwealth Games. As suggested in Derrett (2004), the broader cultural aspects of events bring distinction to the image of a city and its region by enriching them and giving them a unique sense of history and place. In terms of sports events, this ambition commonly becomes manifest in a desire to develop a sporting infrastructure in the form of an elite landmark capital build project. Host organisations and significant decision makers thus acquire an implicit responsibility not only to financiers but also to the host community and relevant social stakeholders for their decisions. The construct of an imagined 'fit' between partners and stakeholders can to some extent be seen as one based upon a temporary marriage of convenience, where decisions concerning the staging of the event and the final veto over crucial aspects of the venue are often made by special interest groups. However, these groups may not always be fully aware of the complexities of risk associated with the financial management and public accountability of the event and venue over the short, medium and long term.

Typically, the economic costs of event generation and facilities construction are offset against their potential community advantages, often subsumed within the umbrella of the event legacy. While this legacy may in part be economic in nature, as for example in the contribution of events to local economic regeneration (Gratton and Taylor, 2000), it is invariably also couched, as can be seen to good effect in the bid for the London 2012 Olympics, in social terms of the projected post-event community use of facilities and venues. Indeed, Gursoy et al (2004) found that event organisers' perceptions of the benefits of events tended to focus on the social rather than the economic. However, such community benefits tend by their nature to be longitudinal, imprecise in predictability and difficult to quantify. Strategic event management, which must inherently embrace post-event impacts, is thus a complex process driven by economic, political and social factors, requiring careful strategic planning. There are, however, competing models of strategic management and planning for events. In an analysis of the planning processes for the 1991 World Student Games in Sheffield, Bramwell (1997b) outlined three theoretical perspectives on strategy. The classical strategy espouses a rationalist approach grounded in the determination of strategic goals followed by the development of planned action to achieve these. The processual perspective adopts a more realistic approach in accommodating a flexibility to react to unforeseen changes of circumstance while the systemic perspective sees planning as "embedded in society's social, economic and political structures", shaped by political and sociological forces. Concluding that all three had in varying ways been brought into play in the planning of the World Student Games, the author outlined a number of potential lessons for future event planners. More recent experience suggests that these lessons have not always been heeded.

This paper addresses some of the above issues through an analysis of the development of the Bolton Arena, a large scale sports venue which was opened in 2001 through partnership development and funding. In particular it explores the impact of two events, the Manchester Commonwealth Games of 2002 and the National Tennis Championship, on the expectations, ambitions and decisions of key members of the Arena's development partnership and the post-event significance of this impact. It also aims to evaluate the nature of the strategic planning process which led to the construction of the Arena. The research was conducted through an examination of documentary sources and through semi-structured interviews with members of the Arena's governing body and with a number of local government officers who had been involved in its development.

The development of Bolton Arena

The history of the Arena provides a revealing case study of the effects of opportunism and risk taking in contemporary large scale sport and leisure development. It also exposes the strengths and weaknesses of cross-sector partnership working. Although the Manchester Commonwealth Games exercised an eventual influence on the design and intended function of the Bolton Arena they were not a factor in its initial conceptualisation in the late nineteen-eighties. The original rationale of the Arena was grounded in Bolton Metropolitan Borough Council's wish to establish a major tourist attraction to raise Bolton's regional profile. The preferred form of this was a sport village, similar in concept to that established at Norwich, located at a site five miles to the north of the town. This was to include a sport and leisure facility that would serve the local community and its development was an integral element of a contemporary re-structuring of local authority sport facility provision in Bolton. Simultaneously, in the wake of the Taylor Report (1989), Bolton Wanderers Football Club was exploring the development of a new ground to replace the decaying inner urban Burnden Park. There was also interest in the development of a large scale urban fringe leisure and retail park to service communities from Bolton and surrounding localities. In 1991 an embryonic partnership of public and private sector organisations, which included the Emerson Group property development company, formed to commission a feasibility study which led in 1994 to the creation of a business plan for the construction of a sport and retail development in which a new football stadium would provide both a home for Bolton Wanderers and public leisure and fitness facilities. Local authority funding was obtained through the sale of public land attached to the site and through the concurrent re-structuring of sport and leisure facilities across the borough. The partnership's strategic aim of building a major sport tourism facility necessarily led Bolton MBC to seek as a partner a major sport governing body to validate a bid for lottery funding for capital building.

The progress of the development of the Arena from this point onwards was determined by two factors, the one an unexpected opportunity for a sport based partnership, the other an announcement of a regional major sports event. The need for a principal sport governing body as a partner was resolved through the fact that in 1995 the Lawn Tennis Association was in the process of developing regional centres of excellence. Although there had been no initial intention that the Arena would be designed as a tennis facility — as stated above it had been conceived as a multi sport centre — the opportunity to gain a partner led the council to approach the Association to locate a regional centre in Bolton. However, the necessary funding remained to be secured. On Manchester's successful bid to host the 2002 Commonwealth Games the partnership realised that lottery funding was likely to be available if the Arena could serve as a venue for the Commonwealth Games badminton competitions. A revised lottery bid was approved by Sport England and funding was released on the basis that the Arena would function as a regional tennis centre, be actively supported by the Lawn Tennis Association, and provide a venue for the Commonwealth Games that would be within the Greater Manchester region but not in that city itself. The imminence of an event was thus crucial to the decision to build the Arena. With funding from Sport England (£11 million Sports Lottery), Bolton MBC (land to the value of £3 million) and the Lawn Tennis Association (£1million), the Bolton Arena was built at a cost of fifteen million pounds and opened in April 2001. Its design was influenced primarily by the new vision of the facility as a major competition and elite performance facility with eight full size indoor tennis courts, a seating capacity of 5,000 spectators and an infrastructure that could accommodate both national and international competitions. It served as an event venue for both the Commonwealth Games and for two national tennis championship competitions.

The post-event phase of the Arena's history illustrates not only Roberts' contention (2004: p. 118) that facilities built to accommodate events are unlikely to be what would have been constructed had they been built primarily for community use but also shows that partnerships assembled to allow such facilities to come into existence may have little overall appreciation of or concern for their function after the event. The Lawn Tennis Association exercised a dominant influence in setting the Arena's operational aims and objectives and despite being the minor partner in terms of capital funding it retained a disproportionate degree of control over the use of the facility. Some element of community use was realised through an indoor tennis initiative which sought to enhance local participation in tennis. However the principal portion of its work was not community orientated and was based upon the provision of the Lawn Tennis Association north west regional tennis programme which sought to enhance the performance levels of elite tennis players, with local high school places being secured for some younger players, and the promotion of an international competition tennis facility. In addition to the indoor tennis facilities the Arena had 6 outdoor American fast dry clay tennis courts, constructed on land that had originally been intended for different sports. It also provided office accommodation for the Lawn Tennis Association on a twenty one year contract. The future of the Arena as a tennis venue was widely acclaimed, with one newspaper report noting that:

> British tennis will soon have a new custom-built indoor arena suitable for staging Davis Cup ties, international tour events and the National Championships while also catering for players of all levels from casual to international training squads. (Roberts, 2001: p. 23)

The Arena operated as a Leisure Trust with a Board of Trustees comprising representatives of the partner organisations involved in its development. However, the Lawn Tennis Association retained a veto on the tennis facility programming and the use of the indoor courts was thus restricted exclusively to tennis, including the two national championships which took place at the Arena. However early in 2002 the Lawn Tennis Association adopted an unexpected and radically divergent strategic approach to the development of British tennis and informed Bolton Arena of its intention to close its north west regional centre (the Arena Board first heard of this on the radio) following which the Arena's role as an emergent national indoor tennis venue diminished and its status as a regional tennis centre was undermined.

Following the partial withdrawal of the Lawn Tennis Association the Arena entered a period in which it was able neither to fulfil its original function nor to diversify into a more general community-orientated sports complex. Despite having withdrawn from the original partnership contract the Association retains a strong degree of influence on the operational management of the Arena and it has not been possible to convert the indoor facilities to sports for which there is a known significant community demand, notably football. The annual operating cost for 2004–5 was approximately £2 million, of which income from tennis was predicted to provide only £300,000 (15%). The Arena has been obliged to re-negotiate an extended subsidy from Bolton MBC to allow it to revise its strategic plan and to become self sufficient within 5 years, primarily through a gradual progression to the provision of other sport and fitness activities. It became possible in late 2004 to change the use of the indoor tennis courts to non-tennis purposes such as badminton and bowls and a number of the American clay outdoor courts have been redeveloped into 5 a side football courts. It has recently staged sport and entertainment events including a televised boxing tournament, featuring Amir Khan, and the Comedy Club. However the change from a specialist elite tennis competition to the community sports facility that was originally envisaged has been fraught with challenges and obstacles, not least the need to alter the perception of the local community, arguably a justifiable one in the light of the Arena's launch publicity, that the venue is not for them.

Discussion

The development of the Arena depended principally on the five factors described above, namely:
- The town council's wish to raise its profile through a sport / tourism development
- The strategic restructuring of leisure facility provision by Bolton MBC
- Sport England's responsibility to allocate lottery funding to major capital sports projects
- The strategic aims of the Lawn Tennis Association
- The imminent responsibility of Greater Manchester to provide world class venues for the 2002 Commonwealth Games

This paper argues that the principal capital funding of the Arena was primarily driven by the event of the Manchester Commonwealth Games which exercised a distorting effect upon the formulation of the partnership's strategic vision and that although there were several contributory factors to the development of the Arena, the need for an international event venue was critical in the decision making process. The event and the facility share a symbiotic relationship in that the event influenced the political decision to build the facility which in turn enabled the event. However, the national and international sports organisations whose drive and support enabled the Commonwealth Games and thus the design of the Arena, have little or no enduring responsibility for its post event survival. Indeed, the partnership was arguably doomed to failure from the outset because it did not comply with the basic imperative, outlined by McFee (2002: p. 13), that all partners should share the same aims or goals. The Arena was funded on the basis of a shared partnership vision, or in Heitzmann's (1999: p. 20) phrase, "an imagery of cooperation among a range of constituencies" which evaporated upon the re-focusing of the Lawn Tennis Association's strategic direction away from the original partnership vision. While it may be an overstatement to suggest, as do both Eckstein and Delaney (2002) and Heitzmann (1999) in relation to event facilities elsewhere, that the post-event community functions of the Arena were simply a social construct to legitimate the bid for funding it may nevertheless be suggested that neither were they clearly articulated nor were all partners structurally accountable for fulfilling their long-term commitment. This may be partly explained through the nature of the planning partnership. As Rowe and Devanney (2003: p. 376) note, partnerships devised for social and economic regeneration purposes are increasingly somewhat artificial, frequently bringing together autonomous organisations for a specific purpose. Those assembled to deliver both sport events and their related venues and facilities generally fall within this categorisation. However, as Rowe and Devanney (2003: p. 381) also note, partnerships are rarely an association of equals and thus partners with substantial resources, or those which are within the partnership because they give it validity even though they may contribute only a small proportion of the funding, may dominate the agenda. It is not difficult to transpose these observations to the development of the Arena.

In terms of its strategic planning, the history of the Arena suggests that event planning became more rather than less complex in the last decade of the twentieth century. The classical perspective which characterised the formulation of the original vision was quickly disabled by changed circumstances and the political pressure to include in the partnership, as a matter of expediency, a sport body with no apparent long-term commitment to significant levels of community use, arguably resulted in an irrational intertwining of partners with vastly differing expectations. Instead, the strategic planning of the Arena appears to be more readily explained by the systemic perspective as rational planning was subverted by unforeseen external factors, primarily the political ambitions awakened by the announcement of the Commonwealth Games, opportunism and alliances built on sand. The notion of SMART (specific, measurable, achievable, realistic and time based) targets, long assumed to be the bedrock of rational planning and decision making, appear to have been not only inadequate but anachronistic in what was essentially a post-modern setting. Mindful of this emerging context, Laybourn (2004) argues that risk assessment is now a major aspect of strategic planning, and the authors of this paper would suggest that not only the assessment but the management of risk, uncertainty and unpredictability are now inherent to event planning and facility-related venue construction. In short, this is the model within which major sports venues come into being.

Conclusion

While the Arena fulfilled its short-term function as an event venue, its ability to do so detracted significantly from its potential to become a community orientated facility after the event. The fracture in continuity between the event and the facility's post-event status may be extrapolated to a series of dichotomous tensions between the event and the post-event viability of the facility (see Figure 1). Although these tensions clearly do not constitute a narrative for all event facilities they nevertheless highlight the potential fractures between the temporary nature of the facility as an event venue and the long term function of the facility as a community venue. In ensuring the availability of a venue fit for the purpose of the event, sacrifices have to be made in the acceptance of a facility that has not been purposely designed for continuing community use. Although one cannot exist without the other, they remain uneasy bed fellows.

The proximity of a major sport event in the guise of the Manchester Commonwealth Games appears to have distorted the original vision of the Arena. The Sport England lottery grant, without which the Arena could not have been built, was rationalised principally by political need

EVENT	FACILITY
Acts as a catalyst for the development of facilities	A major event invokes a vision of a world class facility
Needs facilities to function	Needs event to secure political support and funding
Temporary	Permanent
Articulates the short term function the facility	Long term community function of may not be an event partnership priority
Fit for the purpose of the event	Not necessarily appropriate for post event community use
Has a short term international / national user community	Has a long term local user community
No enduring responsibility for the post event use of the facility	Local management must deal with legacy of the event
Engages a wide range of partners	Post event function engages a restricted range of partners

Figure 1   Dichotomous tensions between event and post-event viability of the facility

to ensure that there was sufficient sporting capital in Manchester to accommodate the Games. The prospect of the Games can thus be argued to have fundamentally changed the originally intended form of the Arena and to have exercised a deleterious effect on its community benefit.

References

Bonney, N. (2004) 'Local democracy renewed?', *Political Quarterly* Vol. 75, No. 1: pp. 43–51.

Bramwell, B. (1997a) 'A sport mega-event as a sustainable tourism development strategy', *Tourism Recreation Research* Vol. 22, No. 2: p. 13–19.

Bramwell, B. (1997b) 'Strategic planning before and after a mega-event' *Tourism Management* Vol. 18, No. 3 pp. 167–176.

Derrett, R. (2004) Festivals, events and the destination, in Yeoman, I. et al. (eds.) *Festival and events Management: An international arts and culture perspective*, London: Elsevier, pp. 32–50.

Eckstein, R. and Delaney, K. (2002) 'New sports stadiums: community self–esteem, and community collective conscience', *Journal of Sport & Social Issues* Vol. 26, No.3: pp. 235–247.

Gratton, C. and Taylor, P. (2000) *Economics of sport and recreation*. London: Spon, pp. 179–192.

Gursoy, D., Kyungmi, K and Muzaffer, U. (2004) 'Perceived impacts of festivals and special events by organizers: An extension and validation', *Tourism Management,* Vol. 25, No. 2, pp. 171–181.

Heitzmann, J. (1999) 'Sports and conflict in urban planning: The Indian National Games in Bangalore', *Journal of Sport & Social Issues* Vol. 23, No. 1: pp. 5–24.

Independent (2005) 7th July: pp. 4–5.

Kronthaler, F. and Franz, P. (2003) 'Methods and problems of assessing regional economic effects of large sports events: Using the Leipzig region's arrangements for the 2012 Olympic Games as a case in point', *Tourismus Journal* Vol.7, No. 4: pp. 439–455.

Laybourn, P. (2004) 'Risk and decision making in events management', in Yeoman, I. et al. (eds) *Festival and events management: An international arts and culture perspective*. London: Elsevier, pp. 286– 307.

McFee, G. (2002) '"Partnering is such sweet sorrow": Some perils of partnership', in G. Berridge and G. McFee (eds) *Partnerships in leisure: Sport, tourism and management* (LSA Publication no 78). Eastbourne: Leisure Studies Association, pp. 11–26.

Prince, T. (2005) 'Olympic hurdles', *Journal of Commerce*, 4th July: *p.* 1

Prystay, C. and Pringle, D. (2005) 'London wins Olympics with emotional appeal', *Wall Street Journal (Eastern Edition)*, 7th July: *p.* 2

Roberts, J. (2001) 'Tennis: Bolton the 'best in Europe', *Independent* 7th February: p. 23.

Roberts, K. (2004) *The leisure industries*. Basingstoke: Palgrave Macmillan.

Rowe, M. and Devanney, C. (2003) 'Partnership and the governance of regeneration', *Critical Social Policy* Vol. 23, No. 3: pp. 375–397.

Taylor P. (1989) *Interim report on the Hillsborough Stadium disaster: 15 April 1989*. London: HMSO.

SPORT EVENT TOURISM AND INVOLVEMENT BEHAVIOUR OF RESIDENT AND NON-RESIDENT SPECTATORS

Margaret E. Johnston

School of Outdoor Recreation, Parks and Tourism, Lakehead University, Ontario, Canada

G. David Twynam

School of Tourism, Thompson Rivers University, Kamloops, British Columbia, Canada

Sport tourism is an important and increasingly common form of travel during which individuals participate either actively or passively (Ritchie and Adair, 2002). An increase in sport tourism has been noted as an outcome of cultural and economic changes that have encouraged and enabled increased participation (Standeven and De Knop, 1999; Kurtzman, 2001; Bordeau, Corneloup and Mao, 2002). Sport tourism involves travel in order to participate in or observe sport, or to visit a sport attraction (Delpy, 1998). Standeven and De Knop (1999: p. 12) define sport tourism as: "All forms of active and passive involvement in sporting activity, participated in casually or in an organised way for non-commercial or business/commercial reasons that necessitate travel away from home and work locality." The key aspect in defining sport tourism is that sport is associated — either primarily or secondarily — with travel. Sports tourism has increased substantially in recent years, and this reflects both an increase in spectator interest in large scale sporting events and an increase in active lifestyles resulting in sports participation during travel (Green and Chalip, 1998).

Active and passive sports tourism appears to be growing in Canada. Canadian data from the early 1990s show approximately five per cent of domestic travel was sports related (Getz, 1997). In 2001, attending a sports event was part of the tourism experience for 7% of domestic tourists in Canada, 6% of American visitors to Canada, and 10% of overseas visitors. Further, participating in sports and outdoor activities was part of the tourism experience for 37%, 31%, and 29% of these groups respectively (Canadian Tourism Commission, n.d.). Weighill (2002) found that 31.2% of domestic travel in Canada was sports-related, with 82% of this being active sports tourism, 9.9% was related to being an event spectator, and the remaining 8% of sports travel included both active and event participation. Gibson (1998) states that travel for sport and physical activity is among the fastest growing segments in tourism.

Another fast-growing segment of the tourism industry is the special event category. This includes festivals, arts or heritage events, exhibitions, and sporting events, and these extend in their attraction of participants from the local to the international scale. Special events are often seen as vehicles for community economic and social development because of their potential to draw tourists, their tendency to leverage investment in new community infrastructure, and the provision of opportunities for community members to participate as volunteers, service providers, employees, and spectators.

Where sports tourism and event tourism intersect — the special sporting event — is the focus of this paper. It examines a key group of participants from the tourism and community perspectives, event spectators, and explores whether the characteristics of sport tourism spectators are similar to those of community spectators. Sport tourism literature emphasizes the non-resident spectators who have travelled to attend the event. These individuals travel in order to observe sport, often as their primary motivation for travel. Special event literature sees sporting events as a sub-category in which the event is the starting place and the spectator is one of several categories of participants. Given these differing approaches to and perspectives on spectators, it should be instructive to explore explicitly the tourist spectator in comparison to the community spectator. This study examines the characteristics of resident and non-resident spectators at a special sporting event with the intention of identifying similarities and differences between the two groups in order to refine our understanding of sport tourists and of event spectators.

Event tourism as a type of sport tourism

The supply side categories of sports tourism are attractions, resorts, cruises, tours, events and adventure (Delpy, 1998; Ritchie and Adair, 2002). The sport tourism event category includes activities that have the potential to attract large numbers of spectators and participants, and that vary considerably in scale, type of visitor, level of impacts, purpose, and benefit-to-cost ratio (Delpy, 1998). Getz (2003: p. 50) states: "From the destination's perspective, sport event tourism is the development and marketing of sport events to obtain economic and community benefits. To the consumer, it is travel for the purpose of participating in, or viewing, a sport event."

Event organizers and politicians commonly emphasize the positive economic impacts of hosting sports events. The expectation is that new tourism dollars will be generated by the event as spectators travel to view the sport event (Hall, 1992; Getz, 2003). Events will also bring in members of the media, support staff, non-resident volunteers, and the participants themselves (Twynam and Johnston, 2004). Hinch and Higham (2001) describe, among other areas, the research possibilities related to understanding the involvement of tourists with sport in a variety of capacities such as athlete, spectator, coach, management, and official. They suggested a number of areas for research, including socio-demographic variables and travel behaviour, upon which these categories might be distinguished. Higham (1999) provides an excellent summary of many of the differences between sporting mega-events, such as the Olympics, and regular season competitions, such as regional or national championships. The scale of sporting events clearly plays a role in the development of the event, its positive and negative impacts in the community or region, community participation, and the legacy potential. Because of these differences, Higham (1999) argues, these smaller scale sports tourism events have much to commend them to governments and communities in terms of tourism development, an idea reinforced in an empirical study of small-scale football competitions (Gibson, Willming and Holdnak, 2003).

Spectators and participants in sports tourism

A further distinction in types of sports tourism exists between the tourist as spectator and as participant. Hall (1992) defines sport tourism as falling into two categories of travel: for participation or for observation. He further defines those who travel to participate into activity participants, for whom leisure is a goal, and hobbyists or players, for whom competition is a goal. Hall (1992) expresses the implications of these divisions in terms of motivation, behaviour and the social context of the activity, and describes the economic impacts and tourism development associated with both the active and spectator sides of sports tourism.

Spectators generally travel to watch a particular event; they may have some specific link to this activity at home, such as a history of personal involvement in the sport or a family connection. Sport tourists who are active participants may be involved as competitors, recreational participants, volunteers, coaches, referees or judges, and other support staff (Hall, 1992; Gibson, 1998; Standeven and De Knop, 1999; Hinch and Higham, 2004).

Getz (2003) states that little is known about the motivations of those who travel specifically to participate in a sport event and that more research is needed on the differences between participating and being a spectator. Green and Chalip (1998) emphasize the distinct motivations among the various types of travellers involved in sport tourism that relates to sport subculture. A tournament is an opportunity to celebrate being a player (a competitive participant). For competitors, the key attraction is not the place or the people — as with most other tourism experiences — rather it is the opportunities afforded by the competition: "The event itself is more important than the destination" (Green and Chalip, 1998: p. 278). Standeven and De Knop (1999) take a different view and argue that a key element in sport tourism for both spectators and participants is the experience of place.

Gammon and Robinson (2003) describe a conceptual model of sport and tourism that is founded upon the role of sport as a primary or secondary motivation to travel, regardless of whether that participation is active or passive. In either division, categorization into the hard sub-group means that the sport is a competitive activity, while a soft sub-group means that the activity is recreational or leisure-based. This approach emphasizes the importance of motivation in sport and tourism behaviour and suggests the potential for better understanding consumer behaviour, satisfaction and impacts. Gammon and Robinson (2003) state that consumers who travel for recreational sport area are not well studied; yet, Pigeassou, Bui-Xuan and Gleyse (2003) claim that, as sport is not at the centre of this travel, study of the phenomenon goes beyond the field of sports tourism. This point suggests a link to behaviour, motivation and satisfaction in tourism more generally.

Active sport tourists, those who travel to engage in sport as leisure, are more likely to be male, affluent and college-educated (Gibson, 1998; Standeven and DeKnop 1999). These individuals are also characterized by a willingness to travel long distances in order to participate, by participation in active sport tourism into retirement, and by repeat travel activity (Gibson, 1998). Weighill's (2002) analysis of Canadian domestic sport tourists in 1999 reinforces the prominence of males in active sport tourism.

Who participates in sport event tourism?

Research on sport event tourists has been minimal, but some late 1990s data from the U.S.A. indicate a greater proportion of sport tourists are male rather than female, that the family market is large, and that sport event travellers generally are younger than other travellers (Getz, 2003). Based on a variety of national travel studies and event case studies, Getz (1991) generalizes that males are more dominant at sports events and females are more dominant at cultural events. Weighill (2002) reports that 38.2% of all Canadian domestic sport tourists in 1999 were adult males, 35.5% were adult females, and the remainder children. The problem of scarce information on demographics has been addressed to some degree by researchers, though it is important to note that current views indicate that the profile of a sport event tourist will vary according to the type of event and other variables (see Standeven and De Knop, 1999; Nicholson and Pearce, 2000; Hinch and Higham, 2004). Getz (2003) recommends that research priority should be given to improving our understanding of market segmentation for these events.

Standeven and De Knop (1999) describe sport event spectators as either connoisseurs or casual observers. Connoisseurs have extensive involvement in, interest in and knowledge of the sport and attending the event is the purpose of travel. Casual observers are less interested and knowledgeable and have not planned specifically to attend an event while on holiday. Ritchie, Mosedale and King (2002) suggest expanding this distinction into a continuum that recognizes a middle group of passive sport tourists whose involvement and interest might enable them to be termed frequent spectators. A conceptual model developed by Kim and Chalip (2004) to explain why people travel to sports events contains five variables, including event interest and attendance intentions. Kim and Chalip (2004) noted that as past attendance behaviour is linked to current attendance, this is an important aspect of spectator behaviour to examine. A report by Nicholls, Laskey and Roslow (cited in Getz, 1997) found that 75% of visitors at a car race were also participants in the sport and that many also attended other race events. These studies suggest that interest, knowledge, involvement, and attendance considerations should be part of the development of spectator profiles that help explain differences in spectator behaviour.

Ritchie et al. (2002) developed profiles for non-resident spectators at two Super 12 Rugby Union events. It was estimated that at one event 16% of the spectators were non-resident, while at the other the figure was 24%. The majority of these sport tourists were male, highly educated and married/living with a partner. Of the sample, 39.2% identified themselves as avid, 22.6% as frequent, and 38.2% as casual spectators (Ritchie et al., 2002). Further profiling described differences among these three groups on attributes such as involvement in the sport, event attendance, and travel behaviour. The authors conclude that profiling sport tourism segments on the basis of behaviour and motivation can provide insights that are useful in understanding and leveraging tourism benefits (Ritchie et al., 2002).

Who goes to events?

Event research shows that visitors can not be considered as a homogeneous group (Backman, Backman, Uysal and Sunshine, 1995). Using data from a national U.S.A. travel survey, Backman et al. (1995) found that travellers to festivals, special events and exhibitions were more likely, compared to other travellers, to be married, not college graduates, and under 50 years of age. Backman *et al.* (1995) found that certain demographic variables were linked to motivation for attending. For example, younger age groups were more likely to travel for excitement. These results reinforce the call for segmentation studies on the basis of demographics, motivation and activity in order to provide event products and promotion that match the needs and interests of attendee groups (Backman et al., 1995).

Nicholson and Pearce (2000) examined the characteristics of visitors at four special events to determine whether there were common features that identified event visitors. Based on a comparison of profiles, they concluded that event visitors are characterized by difference, not homogeneity, indicating that different events appeal to different audiences. For example, women outnumbered men at three of the four events, these three being community festivals; the exception was an air show, where men outnumbered women. This provides support for the argument put forward by Getz (1991) that males are attracted to sports events and females are attracted to arts and cultural events. In a comparison of resident and non-resident event attendees, the groups were similar in terms of age, sex and occupation at three events. The fourth event, where such distinctions were found, was a wine festival. The proportion of resident and non-resident attendees ranged from half non-residents at the wildfoods festival to 90% non-residents at the air show. Nicholson and Pearce (2000) conclude that the diversity of events clearly plays a role in who attends. Diversity includes not only the nature of the activity, but also the scale, location, and organizational structure. Nicholson and Pearce (2000) recommend further large-scale comparative studies to determine whether there are similarities across events or at the same kind of events.

Formica and Uysal (1996) proposed that there might be differences between within-region and out-of-region visitors at a Jazz Festival in terms of demographic variables, motivation and event behaviour. They found that the out-of-region segment included a greater proportion of young, male and professionally employed attendees.

Krauss (1998) examined the characteristics, behaviour, and perceptions of spectators at waterfront festivals, and reported finding similar results to a number of other festival spectator studies: a larger proportion of males and a majority under 45. It must be noted, though, that a number of other studies show some variation on this, and indeed emphasize the lack of homogeneity among event attendees. Twenty-five percent of the respondents were classified as tourists or non-residents, but demographic differences between the two groups were not explored.

Sport spectators were studied by Kerstetter and Kovich (1997) who undertook an examination of the relationship between spectators' demographic and behavioural characteristics and their involvement in the sport. Using the involvement construct and its dimensions of importance, risk, sign, and enjoyment as their starting point, they measured attitudes toward college basketball and being a spectator. With its focus on spectators, this study was a new application of the construct, and the authors determined a number of significant relationships between behavioural variables and particular involvement dimensions. They concluded that the involvement of basketball spectators might be primarily social, and they also suggested that further studies explore how spectators' experience with the sport related to involvement dimensions and whether involvement changed over time.

Spectator profiles based on sport and event behaviour might aid us in understanding the appeal of sports events for spectators in relation to involvement. Experience with a particular sport or with sports events might help explain spectator involvement and this involvement behaviour might elucidate distinctions among various groups of spectators and spectator behaviour. Participation is a variable that expresses one aspect of experience with sport, while prior attendance expresses one aspect of experience with events. In particular, taking this approach will enable exploration of the connoisseur and casual groupings identified by Standeven and De Knop (1999) and provide a preliminary assessment of how these categorizations might be further developed through application to all spectators.

Given that community spectators may well be more numerous at events than tourists, witnessed by the division of resident to non-resident spectators in the Ritchie et al. (2002) study and as theorized in the literature (e.g. Hinch and Higham, 2004), it is also important to include them in an event spectator study. This paper provides an exploration of resident and non-resident spectators and attempts to define them on the basis of demographics and behaviour. In particular, it assesses differences by determining the demographics, satisfaction, event involvement behaviour, and sport involvement behaviour of resident and non-resident spectators at a major sporting event.

Three specific aspects are examined individually and in combination where possible.

1) Demographics — Do resident and non-resident spectators share the same demographic characteristics?

2) Event Involvement Behaviour — Are the groups similar in terms of their previous attendance at special sporting events? Are there demographic distinctions in event involvement behaviour?

3) Sport Involvement Behaviour — How involved is each group on the basis of current participation and competitive history? Can this be linked to the connoisseur and casual division or the event spectator continuum? Are there demographic distinctions in sport involvement behaviour?

Methods

This study was undertaken in Thunder Bay, Ontario, Canada, a mid-sized town that functions as a regional centre for a large rural area. Thunder Bay has an economic history based on resource extraction-related and transportation industries with gradual diversification into other sectors. It boasts extensive opportunities for residents and visitors to participate in nature-based recreation and outdoor sporting activities. The Nordic World Ski Championships involved about 600 athletes, 800 members of the media, 5,000 non-resident spectators and 60,000 total spectators (Twynam and Johnston, 2004).

Two questionnaires were used for this study: one for resident spectators and one for non-resident spectators. Both questionnaires assessed spectators' involvement in special sporting events and participation in Nordic sports, event activities attended, and satisfaction with the experiences. Demographic questions were also asked. Additional questions for non-residents sought information on their reasons for travel, trip behaviour, their participation in other tourism opportunities in the city, and their satisfaction with those experiences. Additional questions for resident spectators addressed volunteering behaviour and hosting guests during the event. Not all of these areas are addressed in this report.

Research assistants approached potential respondents on-site at a variety of points to cover all activity locations and they met quotas each day for resident and non-resident respondents. Staggered start and finish times were geared towards covering spectators at all competitive and entertainment activities on all days. Questionnaires were completed immediately and returned to the assistants, resulting in 318 usable non-resident and 275 usable resident surveys. Souvenir incentives were available and refusals numbered fewer than 10 in each group. As this was a multi-day event, some selection bias may have occurred in that spectators who attended on multiple days had a greater chance of being selected that did those who attended on one day only.

Results

To enable statistical comparisons, results are segmented primarily into the two groups that are the main subject of the analysis: resident and non-resident spectators. Re-grouping is done secondarily to allow comparisons on other bases. Demographic characteristics are outlined in Table 1 opposite. The groups are similar in all respects, except for sex, where the proportion of females and males in the resident respondents differs significantly from the non-resident group.

Table 2 on the following page describes the reasons of the non-resident spectators for visiting Thunder Bay. Over 80 per cent stated that their reason for visiting the city was to be a spectator at the Nordics. Of the remaining 59 individuals (19%) who stated that being a spectator was not their primary reason for visiting Thunder Bay, 24 gave reasons for visiting that were nonetheless event-related. These included being a volunteer, an official, or a competitor, or working in some capacity at the event. Of those whose primary reason for visiting was not event-related (25 respondents), a third were visiting friends and relatives, and 9% had come to Thunder Bay in order to participate in recreational sport not associated with the event. One person had come to Thunder Bay to be a spectator at another sporting event in the city.

Table 3 describes the special sporting event behaviour of both residents and non-residents by outlining attendance at previous amateur sports events. Statistical differences from t-tests indicate that the percentage of non-residents who had attended an amateur sporting event (61%) was significantly higher than the percentage of residents who had attended such an event (p = .001). A significantly higher proportion of resident spectators had attended Commonwealth Games, and significantly higher proportions of non-resident spectators had attended World University Games and Olympic Games. Attendance at World Cup events and Nordic World Championships was not significantly different between the two groups. It is worth noting the generally high attendance at Olympic Games, World Cup events, and Nordic World Championships. When resident and non-residents spectators are combined, males had significantly higher previous attendance at an amateur sporting event (p = .001).

Table 1   Socio-demographics

	Non Resident %	Resident %
Sex 'sig.=.005	n=313	n=275
female	42	55
male	58	45
Marital Status	n=313	n=274
single/ never married	43	39
married/living together	51	55
divorced/separated/widowed	5	6
other		
Age	n=312	n=274
18-24	26	24
25-34	19	21
35-44	23	20
45-54	20	18
55-64	8	10
65-74	2	1
75+	1	1
Occupation	n=311	n=269
homemaker	3	5
student	27	25
unemployed	2	3
retired	7	7
paid employment	48	51
self employed	11	6
other	3	3
Education	N=306	N=267
some high school	11	15
high school diploma	9	11
some university/college	21	19
university/college graduate	38	36
trade or vocational qualification	7	8
post-graduate degree	13	8
other	1	3

Table 2   Reasons for visiting Thunder Bay (n=318)

	%	n
To be a spectator at the Nordics	81	258
Other Reasons:	19	59
Volunteer at the event	9	5
Working at the event	15	9
Official at the event	14	8
Competitor at the event	3	2
To participate in recreational sport (not at the event)	9	5
Visiting friends and relatives	34	20
Various other	17	10

Table 3   Attendance at an amateur sport event

	Non Resident %	Resident %	Significance
Attendance at an amateur sport event	61 (n=193)	46 (n=126)	.001
Commonwealth Games	7	20	.001
World University Games	12	3	.01
Olympic Games	40	18	.001
World Cup Circuit	59	60	
Nordic World Championships	28	23	

Table 4   Recreational participation in Nordic sports in previous 12 months

	Non Resident %	Resident %	Significance
Participation	87 (n=268)	61 (n=145)	.001
Ski jumping	20	11	.001
Classic	90	80	.001
Skate/Free	79	39	.001
Ski-touring	47	24	.001

Table 5   Competitive participation in Nordic competitive events

	Non Resident %	Resident %	Significance
Competitor	54 (n=170)	11 (n=30)	.001
Classic/free relay	64	26	.001
Free	82	57	.005
Classic	87	70	.05
90m Ski Jump	7	0	
120m Ski Jump	5	0	
Nordic Combined	5	3	
Biathlon	18	3	.05
Masters x-country	31	23	

Table 4 describes respondents' recreational participation in Nordic sports in the previous 12 months. Non-residents had significantly higher levels of participation overall as well as in several activities: ski jumping, skate or free-style skiing, and ski-touring. Recreational participation in classic skiing was not significantly different between the groups. In both groups combined, males had a significantly higher rate of participation (p = .005).

Table 5 outlines respondents' competitive participation in Nordic sports. Overall, non-residents had significantly higher participation in competitive Nordic events. In particular, they had significantly greater participation in Classic technique, Free/Skate technique, Biathlon and Classic and Free relay events.

Respondents were re-grouped in order to assess possible distinctions on the basis of attendance at prior events. For simplicity of analysis two sub-groups were used: those who attended prior events and those who had not; this provides a 54—46 % split of the respondents. Table 6 describes the recreational participation frequency for the three more common Nordic sports on the basis of respondents' prior event attendance. Frequency categories were collapsed into two groupings: more (7 or more times in the previous 12 months) and less (6 or fewer times in the previous 12 months). Ski jumping was not included in this analysis because of low numbers of participants. Whether attendance was related to being a competitor was examined. Competitors were more likely to have previously attended an amateur sporting event as a spectator (p = .05).

Table 6   Recreational participation

	n	Less than 6 times %	7 or more times %
Traditional/classic			
Attended other events	293	53	47
Did not attend	244	69	31
Free/Skate technique			
Attended other events	293	57	43
Did not attend	244	70	30
Ski touring			
Attended other events	293	83	17
Did not attend	244	90	10

Discussion

Event involvement behaviour: Differences in attendance behaviour between residents and non-residents might be indicative of distinctions that relate to sport event spectator categories. Though a greater percentage of resident spectators had attended Commonwealth Games (reflecting perhaps both cultural and location-specific access), non-resident spectators had greater attendance at the World University Games and Olympic Games. Event involvement behaviour of the non-resident spectators was generally high for the Olympic Games, World Cup events, and the Nordic World Championships. Further, the percentage of non-residents who had attended any amateur sporting event was significantly higher than the percentage of residents who had attended such an event. These results provide some indication that non-resident spectators could fit the grouping of connoisseur outlined by Standeven and DeKnop (1999). Over 80% of the non-resident spectators travelled to Thunder Bay specifically to attend the Nordic World Ski Championships as a spectator and a further 10% travelled in order to take part in the event in a more active role. According to Standeven and DeKnop, attending the event is the purpose of travel for connoisseurs. Travel for a small proportion of non-resident spectators was not motivated primarily by attendance at the event and this group might be seen as representing the casual observers category. In accordance with the literature and available travel statistics, a higher proportion of males had previously attended an amateur sporting event.

Sport involvement behaviour: Differences are evident between the two groups of spectators on a variety of measures. Non-resident spectators are considerably more involved recreationally in Nordic sports activities and have significantly higher participation levels in competitive Nordic events. These differences suggest that a higher proportion of non-resident spectators can be classified as connoisseurs because of these significant differences in recreational and competitive participation in Nordic ski activities. Using the Ritchie, Mosedale and King (2002) continuum would define some of the resident spectators as frequent spectators, though a much higher proportion would be considered as casual spectators based on their recreational and competitive participation. A higher proportion of males had participated in a Nordic activity recreationally in the previous 12 months.

Conclusions and recommendations

This paper has identified spectator sport and event involvement behaviour based on previous attendance at sporting events and current participation and competitive history. The results indicate that non-resident spectators at the Nordic World Ski Championships are significantly more involved than resident spectators in the event and the sport, and that there is a higher proportion of males in the non-resident group. Nonetheless, Nordic activities are popular with a strong competitive and recreational expression for resident spectators. For both resident and non-resident spectators there were high levels of recreational and competitive behaviour. The spectators in this study were not only fans but also participants. If there is a sports event subculture, as suggested by Chalip and Green (2001), the subculture is not based simply on spectating behaviour, but also on recreational and competitive involvement in the activities and the event.

To gain a greater understanding of spectator behaviour, we need to go deeper into who these people are and why they attend events — how events intersect with their lives more generally. Further research is required that explores passive sport tourism using the enduring involvement concept. Enduring involvement scales have four dimensions: importance, enjoyment, self-expression, centrality (Park et al., 2002). McIntyre (1989) suggested that enduring involvement be viewed as the personal meaning or affective attachment that an individual has for an activity. Havitz and Dimanche (1997) proposed that enduring involvement is about motivation, arousal or interest. Further study of the differences and similarities of sport tourism spectators, with respect to their behaviour patterns, sport, recreation and leisure experience and participation is suggested.

References

Backman, K., Backman, S., Uysal, M. and Mohr Sunshine, K. (1995) 'Event tourism: An examination of motivations and activities', *Festival Management and Event Tourism* Vol. 3: pp. 15–24.

Bordeau, P., Corneloup, J, and Mao, P. (2002) 'Adventure sports and tourism in the French Mountains: Dynamics of change and challenges for sustainable development', *Current Issues in Tourism* Vol. 5, No. 1: pp. 22–32.

Canadian Tourism Commission (n.d.) 2001 Tourism highlights. http://
    www.canadatourism.com/ctx/files/Research_Files/F_F_
    Brochure2001.pdf

Delpy, L. (1998) 'An overview of sport tourism: Building towards a
    dimensional framework', *Journal of Vacation Marketing* Vol. 4, No.
    1: pp. 23–38.

Formica, S. and Uysal, M. (1996) 'A market segmentation of festival visitors:
    Umbria Jazz Festival in Italy', *Festival Management & Event Tourism*
    Vol. 3: pp.175–182.

Gammon, S. and Robinson, T. (2003) 'Sport and tourism: A conceptual
    framework', *Journal of Sport Tourism* Vol. 8, No.1: pp. 21–26.

Gandhi-Arora, R. and Shaw, R.N. (2002) 'Visitor loyalty in sport tourism:
    An empirical investigation', *Current Issues in Tourism* Vol. 5, No.
    1: pp. 45–53.

Getz, D. (1991) *Festivals, special events and tourism*. New York: Van Nostrand
    Reinhold.

——— (1997) *Event management and event tourism*. New York: Cognizant
    Communication Corporation.

——— (2003) 'Sport event tourism: Planning, development, and marketing',
    in S. Hudson (ed) *Sport and adventure tourism*. Binghampton: The
    Haworth Hospitality Press, pp. 49–88.

Gibson, H.J. (1998) 'Active sport tourism: Who participates?', *Leisure Studies*
    Vol.17: pp. 155–170.

Gibson, H.J., Willming, C., and Holdnak, A. (2003) 'Small-scale event sport
    tourism: Fans as tourists', *Tourism Management* Vol. 24: pp. 181–190.

Green, B.C. and Chalip, L. (1998) 'Sport tourism as the celebration of
    subculture', *Annals of Tourism Research* Vol 25, No. 2: pp. 275–291.

Hall, C.M. (1992) 'Review. Adventure, sport and health tourism', in B.Weiler
    and C.M. Hall (eds) *Special interest tourism* London: Belhaven, pp.141–
    158.

Havitz, M. and Dimanche, F. (1997) 'Propositions for testing the involvement
    construct in recreational and tourism contexts', *Leisure Sciences* Vol.
    12: pp. 179–195

Higham, J. (1999) 'Commentary — Sport as an avenue of tourism
    development: An analysis of the positive and negative impacts of
    sport tourism', *Current Issues in Tourism* Vol. 2, No. 1: pp. 82–90.

Hinch, T.D. and Higham, J.E.S. (2001) 'Sport tourism: A framework for research', *International Journal of Tourism Research* Vol. 3, No. 1: pp. 45–58.

Kerstetter, D. and Kovich, G. (1997) 'An involvement profile of Division I women's basketball spectators', *Journal of Sport Management* Vol.11: pp. 234–249.

Krausse, G. (1998) 'Waterfront festivals: A spectator analysis of event tourism in three New England cities', *Festival Management & Event Tourism* Vol. 5: pp. 171–184.

Kurtzman, J. (2001) 'Tourism, sport and culture', *Proceedings of the 1st World Conference on Sport and Tourism*, Barcelona, 22–23 February, pp. 99-110.

Nicholson, R. and Pearce, D.G. (2000) 'Who goes to events: A comparative analysis of the profile characteristics of visitors to four South Island events in New Zealand', *Journal of Vacation Marketing* Vol. 6, No. 3: pp. 236–253.

Park, M., Yang, X., Lee, B., Jang, H–C., and Stokowski, P. (2002) 'Segmenting casino gamblers by involvement profiles: A Colorado example', *Tourism Management* Vol. 23: pp. 55–65.

Pigeassou, C., Bui-Xuan, G. and Gleyse, J. (2003) 'Epistemological issues on sport tourism: Challenge for a new scientific field', *Journal of Sport Tourism* Vol. 8, No. 1: pp. 27–34.

Ritchie, B. and Adair, D. (2002) 'Editorial: The growing recognition of sport tourism', *Current Issues in Tourism* Vol. 5, No. 1: pp. 1–6.

Ritchie, B., Mosedale, L., and King, J. (2002) 'Profiling sports tourists: The case of Super 12 Rugby Union in the Australian Capital Territory, Australia', *Current Issues in Tourism* Vol. 5, No. 1: pp. 33–44.

Standeven, J. and DeKnop, P. (1999) *Sport tourism*. Leeds: Human Kinetics.

Twynam, G.D. and Johnston, M.E. (2004) 'Changes in host community reactions to a special sporting event', *Current Issues in Tourism* Vol. 7, No. 3: pp. 242–261.

Weighill, A.J. (2002) 'Canadian domestic sport travel in 1999', in M. Joppe (ed) *Accessing destinations: How do you get here from there?* TTRA-Canada Conference Proceedings, Edmonton. 29 September–1 October.

FOOTBALL'S COMING HOME — AND IT'S NOT FOR BOYS: THE IMPACT OF THE EURO 2005 WOMEN'S FOOTBALL CHAMPIONSHIPS IN THE NORTH WEST OF ENGLAND

Barbara Bell

Department of Sport and Physical Activity, Edge Hill University, Lancashire (UK)

Introduction

This chapter examines the role of the 2005 Women's European Championships for football, in developing the game of women's football and promoting general female sport participation in the English North West region. The form of event legacy examined here is sometimes referred to as 'soft legacy', compared to the hard or more tangible legacy provided by sports facilities or infrastructure usually associated with major sporting events (McCloy, 2002), or the economic impacts, associated with visitor and spectator spending (Pruess, 2004; Gratton and Henry, 2001). As this event was based on the existing facilities provided in various sports arenas across the region, it provided an almost unique opportunity in event evaluation terms. The research on which this chapter is based is the first phase of a larger study into the sporting legacy of the event, which focuses on the North West region, and in one of the hosting areas in particular, Blackburn, Lancashire. This chapter presents some initial findings on the impacts of Euro 2005 on Women's football and discusses the longer term potential for the Championships' wider legacy. The chapter will also examine some of the issues around measuring such impacts on participation and other aspects of evaluation, which this event has highlighted. In the light of the announcement in July 2005 of the awarding of the summer Olympics of 2012 to London, this event represented an important opportunity to learn about such legacy, particularly for an event with multiple objectives and a diverse range of expected outcomes. As women's football is one of the sports London 2012 will be hosting, this research also provided an opportunity to consider what might be the impact of a Great Britain women's team at the Olympics, on female sport participation.

Football — a game of two halves?

History and tradition has long seen women's football as quite distinctly different from the men's game. Football has been split on the basis of sex for well over 100 years. In England, football has been widely considered as a 'male' sport, since it was first codified and organised in the late 19th century. However, as research is increasingly showing, women seem to be reclaiming a previously hidden or forgotten history (Williams, 2003; Williamson, 1991). But, as Williams (2005) has argued, there remains a 'deeply embedded' inequality, encapsulated by the use of the term 'women's football.' More recently, female footballers, previously omitted from the historical records of the sport, have begun to find their voice and document their own, quite separate traditions (Lopez, 1997; Newsham, 1997; Owen, 2005). Such authors have challenged the myths surrounding female football participation:

> Myths which prescribe football as a masculine preserve are an enduring part of English culture. For example, whether male or female, we learn at a very early age that to perform football 'like a girl' is something to be avoided: it is better not to play at all. (Williams, 2003: p. 70)

Such stereotype and myth have combined to hold back the development of the game for women and various authors have examined how this has been challenged and 'tackled' differently across Europe (Scraton *et al.*, 1999) and the rest of the world (Fan Hong and Mangan, 2004; Majumdar and Bandyopadhyay, 2005). Therefore, football has presented many challenges to females interested in competing and playing at the highest level, or even in any organised club form, for some time and this remains an area of some concern:

> A defining feature of women's football is that it continues to
> be characterised by a struggle for space in the broadest sense.
> (Williams, 2003: p. 69)

There is also a growing body of literature that examines the role that
women's football has played in challenging stereotypes of femininity, or
traditional gender constructs is sport (Shughart, 2003; Cauldwell, 1999;
2003). There is some debate as to how such stereotypes have continued
to restrict both media coverage and spectator interest in the sport as well
as trivialise the efforts of women to perform at the highest levels in this
'masculine' sport (Shughart, 2003).

These social traditions and stereotypes are perhaps more acute in
England compared to the US however, where football is seen as more
acceptable for females, boosted by Olympic and World Cup success
(Shughart, 2003). Despite this, there remain significant differences in the
experiences of females versus males in the sport:

> For women to enter the powerfully male-defined and controlled
> world of football, they have had to challenge dominant notions
> of 'appropriate' female sport. (Scraton *et al.*, 1999: p. 101)

The fascinating story of women's football in England could be summarised as one of resilience, resurgence and re-growth. As Newsham (1997),
Williams (2003) and others have more recently documented, women's
football had tremendous popularity, both for players and spectators, up
to 1921. It was dismissed by the Football Association (FA) as being
'unsuitable' for women and not to be encouraged, so was banned from
grounds affiliated to them. However, women did not give up their sport
and continued to play throughout the mid 20th century, without the
support of the FA. At this time, football was organised by and for
women, headed by the Women's Football Association (WFA). One of the
most famous teams dating back to this era was Dick, Kerr's ladies in
Lancashire (Newsham, 1997, Williams, 2003; 2004). Lopez (1997)
described how the England women's team was established, once the FA
recognised the sport, from the 1970s to the 1990s, due to resurgence in
interest in the women's game after the 1966 World Cup. This was
through the work of the WFA, independent of the FA. Eventually in 1993,
the FA took over the running of football for women and albeit belatedly,
began investing in the growth of the game at the grass roots and elite

levels. The success of the re-growth since 1993, when the FA took responsibility for the running of the female game has been, by any standards, phenomenal. In comparison to other team sports, this was seen as bucking the participation trend for females over the same period (Rowe, 2004). Scraton *et al.* saw this growth as part of a wider social and political trend for female equality:

> Women's access to football can be seen as a political outcome of liberal-feminist discourse that centres on equal opportunities, socialization practices and legal/institutional reform. (Scraton *et al.*, 1999: p. 99)

Football's growth and resurgence in female participantion since 1993 may be considered the result of several favourable factors, rather than evidence of the singular efforts of the FA, or of general moves towards greater social equality. Firstly, the recognition by sport agencies that female participation needed better targeting (Sport England, 1993) led to specific funding for interventions using football as a vehicle. Secondly, the concurrent recognition that coaching-led youth programmes were needed to develop greater infrastructure for sports participation in selected sports (National Coaching Foundation, 1993). Hence, football was one of the sports chosen by many local authorities for activity programmes to promote girls participation in sport. Other local authority-based schemes such as Champion Coaching and its successor scheme, Active Sports, selected girls football for inclusion into coach development programmes throughout the 1990s and up to 2004 (Bell, 2004). Consequently, girl's football has benefited from over ten years of additional investment from various agencies, alongside the FA. Thus the 'sporting capital', of skills, expertise and club infrastructure for the women's game has grown considerably. However despite this growth, football in England remains a deeply divided sport, where gender equity in both power and resources has yet to be achieved, particularly in the Football Association itself, across all levels of the sport (Williams, 2003; Burns, 2005). Despite the fact that football is now recognised as the leading team sport for females with over 150, 000 players, females still only represent 10% of those registered by the FA (FA, 2003).

It was against this backdrop of history and growth that the North West was given the opportunity to host the UEFA Women's Championships in June 2005. As home of the famous Dick, Kerr's Ladies, and reprising the theme of the Euro 96 event for the men, football was certainly, 'coming home', but this time not it was not just for 'the boys', but to what would be described by Lennart Johannson of UEFA as the 'motherland' of football (UEFA, 2005).

The Euro 2005 Championships — background and context

This was a major event, being the largest female only sport event seen in the country and the biggest ever European football event for women, as shown in Figure 1 (UEFA, 2005). However, this chapter is primarily concerned with the long-term legacy of this event on hosting communities, individuals and the sport. Specifically we are concerned with examining the evidence of these impacts and whether we can draw from them lessons for subsequent sports events looking to develop lasting legacies.

Women's Euro 2005 Championships Facts

2005 was the sixth UEFA European Women's Championships

The tournament ran from 5-19th June 2005, in the North West region of England

Venues: Blackpool, Blackburn, Manchester, Preston, Warrington

The tournament involved 8 Qualifiers in 2 groups

    A: England, Sweden, Finland, Denmark

    B: Germany, France, Norway, Italy

Semi-finals included the top 2 teams from each group: Finland V Germany, Sweden V Norway

Final: Germany V Norway at Blackburn (19th June)

Germany were the winners, for the fourth time since 1989.

All England games televised live on BBC.

All games covered by Eurosport Channel for satellite TV across Europe and the world

Source: www.UEFA.com

Figure 1: **Euro 2005 Championship**

Legacy and Events

Essentially, the concept of legacy means that, according to Corbett (2004), a sporting event leaves its community better off than it was before. As was found with the 2002 Commonwealth Games (Manchester 2002 Ltd, 2002), such a legacy can have physical impacts, for example, new facilities or infrastructure, or 'soft' legacy in the form of programmes or personnel, in volunteers or increased employability, or capacity to contribute to sport through experience or training. Unfortunately evidence of the latter type of impact is more difficult to measure and thus presents many challenges for evaluation.

Though event legacy in sport often refers to the hard and/or tangible facilities, sporting or infrastructure, left behind after events, this was not particularly relevant to this event, as it took place in pre-existing venues and involved no new infrastructure building. However, due to the perceived benefits to society of major events, there is growing interest in the notion of 'soft' legacy and the social and human capital developed in and through such events. Such legacy can be developed through working or even volunteering at events as well as watching or participating in them. This experience results in changes to people and individual 'legacies' of development, in skills, knowledge or attitudes, or changed perceptions of self-efficacy or capability. Human and social capital theory suggests that individuals may see long-term benefits due to their enhanced employment status or personal social capital being developed through sporting engagement, either as a volunteer, member of a club or paid employee (Stolle, 1998; Nafukho *et al.,* 2004; Denny, 2003). In sport, volunteers and a growth in participation and sport infrastructure represent a growth in 'sporting capital', needed to support more participation and better performance structures. The notion of 'legacy' has arguably more resonance in the North West region, due to the Commonwealth Games of 2002, where, though impact studies were completed, there has been less attention to the non-economic or sporting capital legacy (Manchester 20002 Ltd., 2003).

The Euro 2005 legacy programme

The consultants commissioned to devise and deliver the legacy programme were previously involved in similar work at the Commonwealth Games. Building on their experience, the programme included special events and activity relating to football and education at all levels, both for participation and building awareness (e.g. Passport 2005, cheerleading display, fan parks and road shows). Some activities were linked with health or other agencies, and were carried out across the region as shown in Figure 2. They were not all about football or women, but they contributed in some way to the aims of the legacy programme, and they were all geared to building both audiences and a positive environment for the tournament. But significantly, the development officer for women

---

The Euro 2005 Legacy Programme

Commissioned and supported by the FA and Sport England Developed and coordinated by DTP consultants, based in Preston. This was designed to ensure a lasting impact for women's sport as a result of the tournament, The legacy programme had a social focus aiming:

To increase awareness of women's football

To increase participation in women's football and sport generally

To raise awareness of health issues and the contribution sport can make to deliver health programmes

To create a legacy programme extending across the region

There were 6 streams to the legacy programme:

Football and sports development

Education

Volunteers

Health

Tourism, Business and Marketing

Special Events

Steering group comprised SDOs from each of the hosting local authorities, plus three others in the region.

Various funding sources contributed to the programme including NWDA, Football Foundation, Sport England, British Council and the FA.

Figure 2:   The legacy programme

and girls football in Lancashire was not part of the legacy steering group charged with implementing the plan and was therefore largely excluded from both the planning and delivery process. The broader nature of the programme may therefore have contributed to less 'joined up' work relating to football development across the region.

Mapping the expected legacy — methods and approaches to event legacy evaluation

A research programme was developed to evaluate the impact of the event specifically on participation in women's football in the region, comparing hosting areas and others outside the immediate venue catchments. This evaluation drew on the work of Pawson and Tilly (1997), in developing a context-mechanism-outcome (CMO) matrix for the event. An important aspect of this approach was to map out the expected impacts and develop appropriate methods and outcome measures based on the implied 'theory' behind the expected legacy, particularly in personnel and perceptions, both direct and indirect to the event. In a 'Programme — Impact –Theory' approach to the event (Rossi *et al.*, 1999), expected legacy measures thus became potential outcomes. For example, the theory that the event would lead in some way to further developing the women's game, or promoting physical activity and sport more generally, specifically by women and girls, meant that participation in football and sport more generally were outcome measures. The 'mechanisms' of the event were the legacy programme activities and how they worked was mapped-out using the implied theory behind their design. Different contexts were provided by the various geographical, social or institutional contexts in which these programmes operated. However, there were some difficulties with this approach as not all of the activities originally planned actually took place and the delivery of the programme was fraught with difficulty, not least in funding (DTP representative, 2005, *Personal communication*). This is why in the 'realist' approach, it was important to consider how the mechanisms of the event worked and with whom or in what context they actually operated. For example, all the legacy activities involved grassroots or voluntary local support to actually deliver them, as funding was quite limited, and sometimes events operated without any clear funding secured. Key to the FA's view of legacy was that the event should draw in as many people from across and beyond the region as possible, but inevitably, most of the legacy activity was focused in the hosting areas. It was also important from the Sport England perspective to have impact wider than 'just' football, but working with other policy groups such as health or education was not easy, when objectives, timescales and approaches differed. One significant factor was the limited lead time with which to plan events and secure funding in the run up to the event. Importantly, the legacy programme was supported by the North West Development Agency (NWDA). This event and the planned wider legacy activities were seen to be consistent with both the regional plan for sport, in particular in the target to increase participation in sport by women and girls, as well as promote the region as a tourism and sporting destination and so attract more events.

One of the projects, cited as a particular success by the legacy team was the 'Hakka' project, which involved over 800 hundred young people across the region in a dance and performance programme in schools. Schools in the local authority areas were each to adopt a team to devise and perform a welcome 'Hakka'[1]. The final performances were eventually held in the smaller regional athletics stadium in Manchester, in front of hundreds of fans arriving early for the opening game and the families of the performers, as UEFA did not initially authorise it for the opening ceremony. However, on seeing the performances and the interest of both spectators and the media, UEFA invited the schools representing Germany and Norway to perform in front of 21,000 people and millions of TV spectators at the final.

Women's Football — building a new audience or a new participation base?

The FA commissioned market research, which indicated that 85% of girls from age 7–15 took part in *some* form of football activity in May 2003. As many as 65% of girls in that age group were playing football at least once per week, which equated to 1.5 million girls (FA, 2003). But despite the growth and scale of participation noted above, football remains outside the top ten activities participated in by women, where participation is dominated by individual activities such as walking, swimming, keep-fit, yoga cycling and tennis. In the UK, less than 0.5% of women play foot-

ball (UK Sport, 2005). Also, as noted above, only 10% of the FA's registered players are women. For girls under 16, netball has retained its
position as the most popular extra-curricular activity, according to
national youth sport surveys (Sport England, 2003). The FA had
announced their intention to develop a professional league by 2003 (FA,
2001), but such plans had not yet come to fruition. Therefore, there are
conflicting pictures of how popular the sport is for girls and women and
how significant any potential growth may be. An important task for the
FA therefore, was to build an audience for the women's game, necessary
to underpin developments at national level and to support the women's
premier league.

As noted above, the legacy programme used a range of mechanisms
to reach audiences for the event. Certain activities, for example, the
Passport 2005 scheme, provided tickets to Euro 2005 at reduced rates.
There was also promotion of the event at pre-event festivals and competitions across the region to girls already participating in football. However, some events were more directly geared to increasing participation,
through one-off days to introduce the game to girls, or by using funding
to expand existing events to include more age groups for girls. The road
shows that toured the hosting venues in the weeks before the event were
aimed at raising awareness and enthusiasm for the event, as well as to
encourage local people to buy tickets. The event observed at Blackburn
clearly captured the imagination of the young people, as it was enthu-
siastically received by hundreds of children (boys and girls of all ages),
who took part in a range of interactive exhibits and a lucky few were able
to meet some of the England players, who dropped in unannounced to
the event.

Another key mechanism was through the educational packs
distributed to schools, including curriculum materials and event
information packs. Though thousands were distributed, it was too early
to say what the level of use and impact has been, but this was an aspect
we intended to trace through our research later in the year[2]. One of the
problems the legacy team had was a lack of specific funding for a
monitoring and evaluation programme, a common situation in many
sports development programmes.

Measuring increased engagement in football following the Euro
2005 event presented some problems, but was based on two simple
measures: audience figures at the tournament and participation figures

for 2005/6 season. This was based on the numbers of registered players and the enrolment in organised clubs/teams. Television audiences and spectator numbers at the tournament demonstrated whether the legacy programme and FA marketing efforts had succeeded in reaching the intended audiences, and could point to the potential for future growth of the women's game. As noted above, one of the barriers to media representation has been the assumption that the audience for women's football was too small for the broadcast media and this has hampered the sponsorship and marketing potential of women's football. An increase in the numbers involved in coaching, leadership and officiating could also be evidence of an increase in sporting capital. In anticipation of this, the FA provided increased funds for female only coaching programmes during 2004/5. Therefore, in tracing the involvement in events and ongoing activity related to football, though impacts of the event were anticipated to be measurable, problems remained in directly attributing any growth to the Euro 2005 Championships, due to the ongoing work in women's football and the overlap with existing development programmes described earlier. Secondary data on participation was gathered by the county development officer for the sport, but was not available at the time of this writing.

Audiences and the image of the game

As identified above, building audiences was a major aspect of the legacy work as this was crucial to changing perceptions of the women's game. The event was hailed as a success by both FA and UEFA, as such large attendances for England and very respectable figures for other games were achieved, as shown in Table 1 (page following) (BBC Sport, 2005).

The BBC coverage was also very important to demonstrate a potential for a mass TV audience for the game. The England games achieved several million viewers and, at their peak, 20% of the audience for the live Saturday evening game (BBC Sport, 2005). The media and spectator audiences was clearly a major impact of the event, and gave the game a much increased profile when there was no competing male football events or other major sporting events with which to share the limelight. Table 2 (page following) was derived from figures published by the British Audience Research Board (BARB), for the period covering

Table 1   TV audiences for Euro 2005

Week ending	Channel and Programme details BBC 2				
	Ranking	Programme	Format	Day	Audience
5/6/05	13	MOTD2	Live	Sunday	2.47 million
12/6/05	10	MOTD2	Live	Saturday	2.34 million
	20	MOTD2	Live	Wednesday	1.62 million

No other highlight or live programme in top 30 programmes for BBC 2

All were England group games

	Eurosport (digital channel) – British Audiences only				
5/6/05	Euro Championships Women 2005 (ECHW) not in top 10 programmes				
12/6/05	3	ECHW	Live	Saturday	120,000*
(group games)	6	ECHW	Live	Thursday	92,000
	7	ECHW	Live	Monday	91,000
	8	ECHW	Live	Monday	75,000
	9	ECHW	Live	Sunday	71,000
19/6/05	1	ECHW	Live	Wednesday	118,000 (S/F)
	2	ECHW	Live	Thursday	96,000 (S/F)

Final 19/6/05 did not appear in top 10 – programme at 10 achieved audience of 47,000 (game shown live on BBC2)

* England game and other group game shown

Source: BARB figures from www.barb.co.uk, accessed 3/7/05

the event. Unfortunately more detailed audience data was only available commercially and thus not accessible for this study.

The image of the game was arguably helped as the game got 'serious' if somewhat muted coverage (for example, BBC2 rather than BBC1 showed the highlight programmes), during which the mainly female presenters and analysts did not feel the need for constant comparisons to their male counterparts. Our hypothesis for follow up focus groups to be conducted later in the year, was that when girl footballers returned to school after the event, they may have had more respect or support from peers and families, and so were more encouraged to

Table 2   Official Attendances at Euro 2005

Match – group games	Date	Time	Venue	Attendance
Group A				
Sweden - Denmark	Sun 5 June	17.00	Blackpool	<1,500*
England - Finland	**Sun 5 June**	**19.00**	**Manchester**	**29,092**
Denmark - England	**Wed 8 June**	**18.00**	**Blackburn**	**14,695**
Sweden - Finland	Wed 8 June	20.00	Blackpool	<1,500*
England - Sweden	**Sat 11 June**	**18.00**	**Blackburn**	**25,694**
Finland - Denmark	Sat 11 June	18.00	Blackpool	<1,500*
Group B				
Germany - Norway	Mon 6 June	18.00	Warrington	<3,000*
France - Italy	Mon 5 June	20.00	Preston	<3,000*
Italy - Germany	Thur 9 June	18.00	Preston	<3,000*
France - Norway	Thur 9 June	20.00	Warrington	3263
Germany - France	Sun 12 June	15.00	Warrington	3835
Norway - Italy	Sun 12 June	15.00	Preston	<1,500*
Total in group stages				**Approx 87,000**
England Games			**Average**	**23,160**
			Total	**69,481 (59%)**
Semi – Finals				
Germany – Finland	Wed 15 June	18.30	Preston	3,585
Norway - Sweden	Thur 16 June	18.30	Warrington	5,722
Final				
Germany - Norway	Sun 19 June	15.15	Blackburn	21,100
Total **				**117,384****

*   attendance estimated – 10,500 across 7 games without figures reported via UEFA

**   reported by UEFA.com

continue with their sport — or take it up more seriously. This broad 'theory' was supported by the FA promotion '*now go play*', which targeted young women with information about football and local clubs immediately after the tournament. However, it is too early to say if any increases directly resulted from the tournament, or were the inevitable consequence of more than a decade of development work through Champion Coaching, Active Sport and the county partnerships referred to above. According to the Lancashire County FA, participation figures had shown a dramatic increase even prior to the event (Football Development officer, *personal communication*).

Initial impacts and issues

Early investigations into the event were essentially concerned with the plans and existing programmes of the local areas (football development). Pre-event interviews with football development officers and other sports development officers raised the issues of the conflicts between centralised plans and local implementation, and often referred to the apparent mismatch between local voluntary effort and expectations of financial support from the FA or Football Foundation. Funding decisions were late in coming and not always favourable, so other funds had to be diverted to support the legacy events or activities, or pre-existing events were 're-branded' to link with Euro 2005. There were also clearly diverse local circumstances. The areas in which the legacy operated varied tremendously. Some areas, steeped in football tradition, like Merseyside and parts of Lancashire, were apparently 'fertile ground' where it appeared there was a better chance of building a legacy than Warrington in Cheshire, for example. This area was considered more difficult for building legacy, as it was considered a Rugby League-oriented community, with no local professional football club, and limited existing football opportunities for girls on which to build. There were also questions about the wider social and political support needed to sustain a surge in interest in the women's game, and whether development of the event legacy was too narrowly focused on the NW. Therefore, against this complex backdrop it was clear that immediate measures alone could be limited in fully exploring the impact of the Euro 2005 event, particularly as outcomes would take some time to establish once the event had been concluded, and there would be problems in attributing any causal link to the event, even if changes were found.

In an attempt to add to knowledge about this sporting legacy, a project was established to examine the impacts of the event in particular parts of the region over a longer period. The initial phase of this project focused particularly on Blackburn and West Lancashire and set out to establish a baseline against which any subsequent changes could be benchmarked and to examine in greater depth what, if any, causal links could be established between the event, legacy activities and the local communities in which they operated.

The 'building a baseline' project in Blackburn and West Lancashire

In line with the realistic evaluation approach of Pawson and Tilley (1997), a mixed method evaluation project was developed, independent of the FA and legacy team, but drawing upon their co-operation for data collection. The project started in March 2005 to provide longer term tracking over 12 months following the event and contribute to the legacy plan for women and girls football in Blackburn and to promote girls football in West Lancashire[3]. This study has also drawn upon secondary data provided by the results of the large scale participation survey conducted by KKP consultants on behalf of the NWDA and sports partnerships in the region (KKP, 2004).

The study gathered both quantitative and qualitative data from a range of relevant sources, including participants, sports development officers, the Football Association and schools. Primary data consisted of interviews and survey, focus groups, field notes on site visits (observations and analysis). The aim of such approaches, within a realist evaluation was to not only describe and attempt to measure subsequent patterns of participation, but to build better understanding of *how* any growth or change was achieved and with whom. Therefore, the project attempted to measure the changes to the nature of football engagement and the impacts on legacy event participants through a small survey. This aimed to establish any changes to the frequency of participation or the development of competitive structures. Qualitative data abut the level of involvement of young female footballers and what this represented both to them and providers of opportunities is of particular interest, because this provides rich data and thus contributes to better understanding of the processes involved. We were particularly interested in *how* the event changed attitudes or perceptions about women's football and whether this was likely to be sustained, through organisational or wider societal changes over time. Over the following year, the project will continue to address the impact of the event, in two distinct areas and in very different communities. This will ultimately contribute to constructing a CMO for the event and its mechanisms; educational resources to schools, the provision of coaching programmes, promotional road shows and other public relations activities. The achievement of particular outcomes can then be linked to local contexts and experiences in very different communities. By such an analysis, it may therefore be possible to draw out conclusions about the nature of 'soft legacy' and how it is built through major sporting events.

West Lancashire was selected as the equivalent of a 'control' in this research design, as it had no links to the Euro 2005 legacy programme and only a limited local infrastructure for women's football. The only specific legacy work was a small scale event by the HE college to promote the tournament to local schools in April 2005. This also enabled a piloting of data collection and analysis methods to be used in Blackburn. Participants at the event, secondary school pupils in West Lancashire, were surveyed in April 2005 about their current involvement in football and their interest in a possible coaching programme at the college (n= 73). A comparative group of pupils from a school that did not take part in the event was also surveyed to compare their views and experiences of football (n=50). This was to be followed during the 2005/6 academic year, by school focus groups and follow up questionnaires, to those indicating their willingness to take part, to see whether their involvement with football had changed and to identify whether they perceived any changes in opportunities or attitudes towards girls football in either schools or their wider communities. An amended version of the event participant questionnaire was circulated at the events run by Blackburn with Darwen council in June 2005 and a similar follow up was planned in a selection of schools across the district. The results from the baseline studies as of July 2005, are briefly summarised below.

West Lancashire and Blackburn — baseline studies results

The survey of participants in the West Lancashire legacy event and non participants showed a clear distinction, between the girls attending the event and those who did not, in their engagement and experiences of football both in and out of school. Table 3 shows that the non-participant group had fewer opportunities in secondary schools and fewer girls were involved in clubs. Of those who played in a club currently, 84% were in girls only clubs (this may have included the after-school clubs) and all of these girls were in the group attending the event. Though there was some interest across both groups in attending the proposed football

Table 3:   Comparison of participants and non participants - West Lancashire legacy event

Where have you played football **this year**	Participant Group % Yes	Non-participant group % Yes
Regularly in PE lessons	97	58
With friends in breaks at school or informally after school	70	28
In an after-school clubs	82	15
At clubs or teams not organised by schools	50	20
Coaching organised by school	72	8
At primary school	88	60
Currently club member	48	none
N=	73	50

coaching programme, this was more pronounced in the group participating in the event, but as they had been selected to take part due to their interest in the game, this was perhaps not surprising. The group who had not taken part in the event were apparently *not* aware of the Euro Championships taking place, despite the same information being forwarded to all schools. This illustrated the importance of the secondary school context on the effectiveness of the mechanisms used to promote the game to girls and reflects the powerful influence of school experiences on potential engagement with football — still clearly perceived by some teachers as not 'gender appropriate'.

In Blackburn, a baseline was established partly through an analysis of the survey of participation in Year 9 (KKP, 2005), which showed that although playing football was one of the most popular sports outside of school for girls, few girls had regular opportunities through their schools. When this survey is repeated in the future, it should therefore be possible to see if the proportions of those involved in organised football have risen or not. In order to gain some insight into the level and nature of their football involvement, the participants at the Blackburn legacy events were surveyed in June, but a disappointing return resulted in a very small group for comparison to the West Lancashire group (44 responses). The results of this analysis are shown in Tables 4 and 5.

Table 4:   Participation in Football - Blackburn event participants June 2005

Where have you played football this year ?	% Yes
In regular PE lessons at school?	64
At break or after school, just with your friends?	73
In an after school club	64
At coaching sessions organised by a school ?	48
Did you play football in your primary school ?	96
Do you belong to a football club at the moment?	68
Is this a girls only club?	75
N= 44	

Table 5:   Context of football participation – Blackburn event participants

Playing football outside of school	% Yes
I play in a club or team every week	73
I sometimes play in a team	43
I play just for fun with my friends, not in a team	36
I play in a league	64
I play in a development centre (coached sessions)	27
I play at an FA Centre of Excellence	4
N=44	

These players showed, as in the West Lancashire group, a pattern of regular participation both formally (in P.E. classes or clubs) and informally, with friends. Also, the players taking part in these summer events were largely already committed to regular, organised football. Therefore, the legacy programme may not have had a major impact on new participants to the sport.

Based on the responses of the participants at later events (August 2005) a further analysis concluded that the opportunities for girls in schools after age 11 could be a major factor in whether girls continued with the sport. However, it was clear that there was not a direct relationship between attending legacy events and subsequent activity levels. Those attending many of the events, particularly those later in the summer, were already playing regular football, regardless of the Championships. However, these players were also more likely to have been to a game than not, and had shown clear awareness of the Euro 2005 event. Focus groups with girls in different schools were subsequently planned to develop a greater understanding of how different school contexts may have influenced attitudes and perceptions of girls towards football, since the event. These will be mirrored in West Lancashire later in the 2005/6 academic year.

Discussion

At this stage in the research process, the initial baseline data collected in Blackburn and West Lancashire has provided cohorts for the longitudinal approach required to establish a link between the mechanisms of the event legacy process and the outcomes achieved. The surveys have also helped to establish the nature and context of football participation by young women in these two areas. What was immediately clear through the research in both West Lancashire and Blackburn was that this was certainly a major and unique sports event, with far reaching impacts for football and women's sport in the region. Though it is too early to be conclusive, it appeared to have put women's football back on the sporting map and onto the radar of the sporting public, given the audiences and spectator numbers achieved. Also it has certainly led, in the short term at least, to an increased impetus for greater research attention for women's sport/ gender and sport issues, as shown by the conference papers at the international conference on women and football, organised as part of the legacy programme by the International Football Institute in June (IFI, 2005). However, it remains to be seen whether Euro 2005 achieved the wider impacts the legacy programme was designed to produce. An important task now is to attempt to place Euro 2005 in the policy cycle for women's sport and assess how important it has been in the long term development of women's football both in England and internationally. This will only be possible once outcomes have had time to develop and may require larger, national surveys, outside of the scope of this study. Longer term impacts on female sports participation may only be measurable through repeating the surveys on a regional basis and comparing rates of growth in the North West with other regions.

Are girls in Blackburn inspired to 'Bend it like Kelly'?

Scraton *et al.* (2005) have noted that we need to know more about the 'everyday experiences' of different sportswomen, particularly how gender, race and ethnicity are interwoven. The tournament clearly raised the public profile of the England 'stars', such as Kelly Smith (featured in *Bend it like Beckham*)[4]. Therefore of particular interest in the Blackburn case, was the response by minority ethnic communities to this women's football event. Blackburn has significant numbers of ethnic minorities in the population, impossible to ignore in a realist evaluation, as this represented an important contextual difference to girls in the West Lancashire area, where ethnic minority populations are much lower.

As women's football experienced a surge of interest after the release of *'Bend it like Beckham'*, some have questioned whether such popular culture attention to football has helped to break down the stereotypes afflicting footballers of all ethnic backgrounds (Scraton *et al.*, 2005; Giardina, 2003). It is suggested by existing research that the response to football of young women is a complex of gender, sexual identity, and ethnicity. We intend to further explore the concepts of sporting pathways and perceptions of young women in the focus groups in our project and follow up surveys in 2006. We wish to examine whether young women enter the game with a view of possible pathways into the elite level, and whether or not this is relevant to different ethnic groups. However, no young women in the initial surveys were from an ethnic minority, despite efforts being made in the sample to try to include them. As suggested by the Sport Commitment model (Scanlan *et al.*, 1993), such opportunities and how they are perceived could be an important factor for greater commitment to a sport and so this model has been the basis of the focus group interview schedules. However, as in other sports, the issues of equity and excellence remain a source of almost perpetual conflict in football, as different aspects of the game require differential funding, and the interests of the talented few may divert resources from the many. An important assumption behind the public support of such major events as Euro 2005 is that the exploits of the top athletes inspire young people to take up sport. This was certainly explicit in the London 2012 presentation to the IOC in 2005. If the multi-ethnic England women's team at Euro 2005 does indeed provide evidence that the opportunities for all those with talent can reach the top in football, it remains to be seen whether young women receive appropriate support in their local communities to facilitate continued engagement. Early indications are that the women's game, in Blackburn and West Lancashire at least, is the domain of the majority white population. But it was also clear, that for the first time, supporters and players of the female game saw their 'heroines' in a major tournament and featured in unprecedented levels on the television. Players previously unknown to many outside of the game, received national prominence at this event. Therefore, based on the initial findings above, the event provided an almost unique opportunity, due to its size and media exposure, to examine whether this assumption could be demonstrated. Young women have seldom seen top female footballers in action, outside of the *Bend it like Beckham* scenario. However, the results appear to be inconclusive so far, and more work on the response to the event by young women in the wider communities is needed.

The particular challenge for research in this area is to link exposure to Euro 2005 in a 'cause and effect' relationship to any changes in attitude or social norms we are able to determine. As the calls grow for football to exploit its popular appeal, Johansson's apparent call for use of female sexuality to sell the game to sponsors could be seen to be sending out 'mixed messages' to young women about their relative freedom of expression in sport (Rudd, 2005). This is encapsulated in the use of images of *Charlie's Angels* on Eurosport posters and Nationwide Building Society's 'more beautiful game' slogan which was arguably using sexualised images of female footballers, to promote greater female participation.

Looking to the future for women's football

It is clear that there is great potential for research on the sponsorship and wider support of and participation in the women's game. With a World Cup qualification ahead, and efforts by the FA to establish the women's premier league, the road leading to 2012 is full of possibilities. But it is clear that the planning needed to capitalise on the impacts of the Euro 2005 must move ahead before all the results of studies like those discussed here can provide definitive answers. The policy research cycle may yet again be seen to move too slowly for the relevant sport policy networks need for information. However, such efforts should nevertheless continue to build understanding and knowledge of these important processes.

There are also wider implications for sport policy, as with longitudinal and realist methods, there is some potential to establish if there is a benefit in sports development and to wider society from such events. However, we need more extensive research into whether this benefit is wider than the (football) game itself, and whether it can be sustained over a longer term. But even at this stage we can suggest that building a legacy in sport development terms is a long term process, as it is based on a cumulative process of human and sporting capital growth, which takes time to be established. Consequently the planning cycle needs to allow time for legacy programmes to be planned and developed across a range of partners and agencies, and their outcomes given time to come to fruition. In women's football this will mean a sustained programme of development work associated with World Cup and Olympic qualification needs to be established in a continual process up to and beyond the 2012 games. It will be interesting therefore to see to what extent this is reflected in the current review of the structure of football by Lord Burns, and the new strategic plan for football, currently under development. Our research, we hope, will contribute to an understanding of how such legacy can be developed more effectively. However, this research has already raised some questions, particularly in the ability of the FA and other agencies to achieve their objectives in diverse communities. There are a range of local and regional agencies at work in these areas, with often overlapping and at times conflicting objectives and approaches and different priorities. If the women's game is to develop, it will clearly require a significant increase in support to the club and voluntary sector, but this is already under pressure to service existing demand. The key question is whether the FA has both the infrastructure and the will to support the anticipated growth in women's football over the next five to ten years. While the women's game in England and Europe remains the poor relation to both the professional and amateur male game, can the women continue to survive on the crumbs from this table? At this stage in our research, it is possible to identify the Euro 2005 event as an important policy watershed, but the challenge for the FA and others now is to build on this for World Cup and Olympic opportunities to come.

Notes

1   This was modelled on the traditional ceremony conducted by New Zealand rugby teams before their games, but intended in this form to be a modern dance, devised by the young people.

2.   At the time of writing, only baseline data had been collected. Schools use of resources was to be followed up at the end of the academic year in June 2006.

3.   The project is funded by Edge Hill Research Development Fund for 2005/6, in partnership with Blackburn with Darwen Borough Council

4.   The feature film 'Bend it like Beckham' was released in April 2002, produced and directed by Gurinder Chada.

References

BBC Sport (2005) 'FA hails Euro 2005 as big success' online at: http:// news.bbc.co.uk/go/pr/fr/-/sport1//hi/football/women/ 4087208.stm, accessed 17th June 2005.

Bell, B. (2004) *An evaluation of the impacts of Champion Coaching on youth sport and coaching'*. PhD Thesis, University of Loughborough.

British Audience Research Board (2005) 'Audience figures for June', online at www.barb.co.uk accessed 3rd July 2006.

Burns, Lord (2005) 'FA structural review: An open letter', online at *http://www.thefa.com*, accessed 26th June 2005.

Cauldwell, J. (1999) 'Football in the UK: Women, tomboys, butches and lesbians' in Scraton, S. Watson, B (eds) *Sport, Leisure Identities and Gendered Spaces* (LSA Publication No 67). Eastbourne: LSA Publications, pp 95–110.

Cauldwell, J (2003) 'Sporting gender: Women's footballing bodies as sites for the re-articulation of sex, gender and desire', *Sociology of Sport Journal* Vol. 20, issue 4: pp371–386.

Corbett, R. (2004) 'The future is bright', Centre for Sport and the Law online at: http://www.sportlaw.ca/articles/other/article13.htm, accessed 2nd August 2005.

Denny, K. (2003) *The effects of human capital on social capital: A cross country analysis.* London: Institute for Fiscal Studies.

DTP Partnership (2005) *Personal communication,* July 3.

Fan Hong, Managan, J.A.(eds) (2004) *Soccer, women, sexual liberation: Kicking off a new era.* London: Taylor and Francis.

Football Association (2001) *The Football development strategy 2001–2006.* London: The Football Association.

Football Association (2003) 'Participation figures', online at http://www.thefa.com/Womens/Reference-FAQ/Postings/2003/11/Participation+Figures.htm accessed on 3rd November 2004.

Gratton, C., Henry, I. (eds) (2001) *Sport in the city: The role of sport in economic and social regeneration.* London: Routledge.

Giardina, M.D. (2003) '"Bending it like Beckham" in the global popular: Stylish hybridity, performativity and the politics of representation', *Journal of Sport and Social Issues* Vol. 27, issue.1: pp. 65–82.

International Football Institute (2005) 'Women, Football and Europe' Conference, Preston June 11–16, 2005. Abstracts online at: http://www.uclan.ac.uk/host/ifi/conference.htm, accessed 27th June, 2005.

KKP Consultants (2005) *Participation in sport and the arts, Blackburn with Darwen.* Unpublished report to Blackburn with Darwen Borough Council.

Rowe, N (Ed) (2004) *Driving up participation: The challenge for sport.* London: Sport England.

Lopez, S. (1997) *Women on the ball.* London: Scarlet.

M2002 Limited (2002) *The lessons learned: Final report.* Manchester: Manchester 2002.

Majumdar, B., Bandyopadhyay, K. (2005) 'The gendered kick: Women's soccer in twentieth century India', *Soccer and Society* Vol.6, issue 2/3 : pp.270–284.

Mc Cloy, C. (2002) 'Hosting international sports events in Canada: Planning for facility legacies', *The Global Nexus Engaged* 6th International Symposium for Olympic Research: pp135–142.

Nafukho, F.M., Hairston, N.R., Brooks, K. (2004) 'Human capital theory: Implications for human resource development', *Human Resource Development International* Vol 7, issue 4: pp. 545–551.

National Coaching Foundation (1993) *Champion Coaching — more recipes for action.* Leeds: NCF.

Newsham, G. (1997) *In a league of their own*. London: Scarlet.

Owen, W. (2005) *Kicking against tradition*. Stroud: Tempus.

Pawson, R., Tilley, N. (1997) *Realistic evaluation*. London: Sage.

Pruess, H. (2004) 'Calculating the regional impact of the Olympic Games', *European Sports Management Quarterly* Vol.4, issue 4: pp. 4–253.

Rossi, P. H., Freeman, H.E., Lipsey, M.W. (1999) *Evaluation: A systematic approach*. Thousand Oaks: Sage Publications.6th Edn.

Rudd A (2005) 'Johansson's view of the future is an indecent proposal' *The Times* online at: http://www.timesonline.co.uk/printfriendly/ 0,,1-27-1658761-27,00.html, accessed 4th July 2005.

Scanlan, T.K., Carpenter, P.J. Schmidt, G.W., Simons, J.P., Keeler, B. (1993) 'An introduction to the sport commitment model', *Journal of Sport & Exercise Psychology* No 15: pp. 1–15.

Scraton, S., Cauldwell, J., Holland, S. (2005) 'Bend it like Patel: Centring race, ethnicity and gender in feminist analysis of women's football in England', *International Review For The Sociology of Sport* Vol 40, issue 1: pp. 71–88.

Scraton, S., Fasting, K., Pfister, G., Bunuel, A. (1999) 'It's still a man's game? The experiences of top-level European women footballers', *International Review for the Sociology Of Sport*, Vol. 34, issue 2: pp. 99–111.

Shughart, H. A. (2003) 'She shoots, she scores: Mediated constructions of contemporary female athletes in coverage of the 1999 US women's soccer team', *Western Journal of Communication* Vol. 67, issue 1: pp. 1–31.

Sport England (1993) *New horizons*. London: Sport England.

Sport England (2003) *Young people and sport in England: Trends in participation 1994–2002*. London: Sport England.

Stolle, D. (1998) 'Bowling together, bowling alone: The development of generalised trust in voluntary organisations, *Political Psychology* Vol. 19, issue 3: pp. 497–525.

Williams, J. (2003) *A game for rough girls? A history of women's football in Britain*. London: Routledge.

——— (2004) 'The fastest growing sport? Women's football in England', in Fan Hong, Mangan (eds) *Soccer, women, sexual liberation: Kicking off a new era*. London: Taylor and Francis, pp 112–127.

——— (2005) Unpublished Presentation to IFI Conference, Preston June11, 2005.

Williamson, D. (1991) *The belles of the ball*. Devon: R&S Associates.

UEFA (2005) Official approval for EURO success. Online at : http://www.
    uefa.com/competitions/WOCO/news/kind=1/newsId=310875.html
    accessed 27th June 2005.

UK Sport (2005) *UK strategy framework for women and sport*. London: UK
    Sport.

THE STORY OF AUSTRALIA: NATIONAL IDENTITY AND THE SYDNEY 2000 OLYMPIC GAMES OPENING CEREMONY

Leanne White

School of Hospitality, Tourism and Marketing
Victoria University, Australia

The importance of Olympic Games Opening and Closing Ceremonies

The Olympic Games is regarded as the 'spectacle par excellence' and the Opening Ceremony is often considered the most important event in the Games telecast. This 16 day period of intense competition staged every four years is anticipated and enjoyed by millions.

Founder of the modern Olympic movement, Pierre de Coubertin, recognised that it was through the enactment of the ceremonies that Olympic ideals were performed and communicated. The ceremonies were the place where the Olympic Games could take on deeper significance beyond athleticism alone and central prominence is deliberately given to the national identity of the host country (Larson and Park, 1993: p. 194). The budget for the Opening and Closing Ceremonies, as well as the presentation of medals for the Sydney Games was AUD$50 million (Cameron, 2000).

In one of the key guides to Sydney 2000 published prior to the event it was explained that the main objective of the Opening and Closing ceremonies was to "reflect and interpret contemporary Australian cultural, social and political values in an outstanding production" (News Limited and Harper Collins, 2000a: p. 14).

The Sydney Games were the second time that Australia had hosted an Olympic event. The first time was in Melbourne in 1956 when the event became fondly remembered as 'The Friendly Games'. At the 1956

Melbourne Olympic Games, 3184 athletes from 67 countries participated in 16 sports. This time around more than three times as many athletes — in excess of 10,300 — from almost 200 countries took part in 28 sporting events (News Limited and Harper Collins, 2000b: p. 3).

The Premier of New South Wales, Bob Carr, announced that the Opening Ceremony was Australia's greatest creative work (Veal and Lynch, 2001: p. 424). Carr proudly stated, "Sydney 2000 is one story nobody need fake. This was Australia on show as never before — an intelligent, friendly, contemporary society" and the Sydney Games were "the biggest and most exciting thing to happen in this nation during peacetime" (Webb, 2001: pp. i–ii). If the Sydney 2000 Games were regarded as Australia's greatest story, the Opening and Closing Ceremonies were considered the bookends (Webb, 2001: p. 96).

Australia's moment in the sun: the Sydney 2000 Olympic Games Opening Ceremony

On 15 September, 2000 Australia staged the most watched television event in its history — the Opening Ceremony of the Sydney 2000 Olympic Games. The Opening Ceremony was beamed to a global television audience estimated at around 3.5 billion (Webb, 2001: p. 94). The official ratings figure recorded that 10,436,000 Australians tuned in to watch the Opening Ceremony on the Seven Network (also known as Channel 7). This was a ratings record for an Australian television program (Warneke, 2000: p. 6). The television ratings figures are even more impressive when one considers that they do not take into account those people who watched the event on giant outdoor screens in public places, in the workplace, and at pubs and clubs. Additionally, an important local audience of almost 110,000 people witnessed the spectacle in a quite different manner within Stadium Australia. The crowd gathered at the venue was the largest in the history of the Olympic Games (Bingham-Hall, 2000: p. 68).

Was the Opening Ceremony well received? Why did many Australians fear that the night might simply turn out to be an embarrassing public display of hackneyed and clichéd Australian images with tired and unimaginative stereotypes? Director of Ceremonies Ric Birch had indeed given Australians good reason to worry when an 11 minute preview of the next games in Sydney was televised to billions at the Closing Ceremony of the Atlanta Games in 1996. Birch came under fire for selecting Aborigines with didgeridoos, cockatoos, Bondi lifesavers and most notably inflatable kangaroos on bicycles when he provided the world with a preview of the forthcoming Games in Australia.

The Opening Ceremony was comprised of 13 segments, with each segment costing around $1 million and involving approximately 1,000 performers — mostly volunteers (Webb, 2001: p. 99). While a limited number of dress rehearsal photographs had been released to a curious media and public, the specific details of the event had been carefully kept under wraps. Those who had previewed the spectacle were sworn to secrecy. The biggest secret of all was who would light the cauldron and, importantly in Olympic Games tradition, how would it be lit?

The important message of reconciliation between black and white Australia was loud and clear for the world to hear. Some have argued that the symbolism was too heavy-handed and was perceived by many as "schmaltzy and tear-jerking" (Lenskyj, 2002: p. 221). If Australians hadn't understood the message when thousands walked across the Sydney Harbour Bridge in May for Corroboree 2000, or managed to comprehend the symbolism of Nelson Mandela holding a young boy from the Yorta Yorta tribe in Melbourne a week before the commencement of the Games, the imagery was made obvious to all on this occasion.

The Opening Ceremony began with a stirring 'Welcome' sequence. This was followed by seven separate themes and individually choreographed segments unveiled on the evening. They were 'Deep Sea Dreaming', 'Awakening', 'Fire', 'Nature', 'Tin Symphony', 'Arrivals' and 'Eternity'. Following these segments, the Sydney 2000 Marching Band took to the arena, then the parade of athletes, official speeches, flag ceremony, reading of the oath for athletes and officials, concluding with the all-important lighting of the cauldron with the Olympic flame.

Methodology

As outlined, this paper is concerned with addressing the question: What symbols and images were engaged to present 'Australia' and the idea of 'Australianness' in the Opening Ceremony of the Sydney Games? This article is interested in exploring how concepts of Australia, Australians and Australianness were created and represented by image makers, particularly in this case Master of Ceremonies Ric Birch. This paper is concerned with examining images of Australia by using particular features of both semiotics and content analysis — key qualitative and quantitative research methodologies.

Some of the Australian signifiers included in the Opening Ceremony were: Akubra hats, Driza-Bone coats, Australian flags, Australian native flora, Victa lawnmowers, the Southern Cross, the performance of the national anthem *Advance Australia Fair,* and Australian songs such as *Waltzing Matilda* and *Click go the Shears.* Australian signifiers which were incorporated into the Closing Ceremony included: a blow-up kangaroo on a bicycle, the Australian flag, Hills clothes hoists, Bondi lifesavers, Australian celebrities such as Kylie Minogue, Elle Macpherson and Paul Hogan, and the performance of Australian songs such as *Island Home, Treaty, Down Under* and again, *Waltzing Matilda.* However, it is the Opening Ceremony which is the focus of this article.

The qualitative methodology of semiotics encompasses the relationship between a sign and its meaning/s, the way in which signs are combined into codes, and the wider culture within which signs and codes operate. Semiotics can be efficiently applied to the analysis of visual texts. Semiotics is also a particularly useful methodology for deconstructing aspects of cultural representations and experiences. As Johnathon Culler notes, "All over the world the unsung armies of semioticians, the tourists, are fanning out in search of the signs of Frenchness, typical Italian behaviour, exemplary Oriental scenes, typical American thruways, traditional English pubs" (Culler in Urry, 1995: p. 133).

According to William Leiss, Stephen Kline and Sut Jhally in their landmark text *Social Communication in Advertising: Persons, Products and Images of Well-Being,* the real strength of semiotics is "its capacity to dissect and examine closely a cultural code and its sensitivity to the nuances and obligue references in cultural systems" (1990: p. 214).

The quantitative methodology of content analysis is concerned with the frequency of content contained in a particular data set. Bernard Berelson defined content analysis as "a research technique for the objective, systematic and quantitative description of manifest content of communications" (Berelson, 1952: p. 15). Content analysis is effectively a counting strategy and is put forward as an objective method for counting content as the end result should be able to be replicated by another researcher.

The aim of content analysis is to produce a relatively systematic overview of a particular data set. It is concerned with "the denotative order of signification" (Fiske, 1990: p. 136). An essential feature of content analysis is the use of categories. When classifying data into categories, the main aim is to reduce the material and detect systematic patterns and structures. Content analysis is therefore primarily concerned with studying what is actually evident on the screen. It does not concern itself with questions of quality or interpretation.

As outlined above, semiotics is a valuable methodology for undertaking a close analysis of a particular text — whether that be a particular shot in a television program, a specific scene, or an advertisement. On the other hand, content analysis is able to perform analysis over a larger sample and thus detect similarities, differences and possible trends. When semiotics meets content analysis, we can interpret key features of the text and also measure the frequency of the specific phenomenon under investigation.

Following the methodology developed by Leiss, Kline and Jhally, this article aims to bring the benefits of both qualitative and quantitative analysis to the understanding of the phenomenon under examination — the use of images of Australia and Australians and representations of Australianness at the Sydney 2000 Olympic Games. In deconstructing images of Australia broadcast at the Sydney 2000 Olympic Games, one can examine what was presented and how these images relate to a wider understanding of Australian culture and an 'Australian story'.

Welcome

While the television viewer was waiting for the Opening Ceremony to commence, it was revealed that the performance area of Stadium Australia had been resurfaced to resemble the colours and texture of the Australian outback. While one could only hazard a guess about the type of performance that was in store, it was clear that the harsh physical aspects of Australia, particularly the desolate and stark iconography of the arid outback, was going to play a central role.

Leading the Opening Ceremony was the Welcome sequence where a lone horseman entered the arena, reared his horse twice, cracked his whip, and was then followed by other stockmen and women riding in formation to the stirring theme music from the 1982 film version of *The Man from Snowy River*. All 120 riders carried a white flag with the five Olympic rings displayed in the aqua blue colour of the sea. This colour was apparently selected because the blue sea unites all nations of the world.

To the delight of the crowd, five teams of 24 horses and riders galloped into the stadium. The Olympic colours of red, blue, green, yellow and black were represented by the riders' scarves. The five groups of riders entered the stadium by forming a line and riding across the arena. They then peeled off to the sides of the arena and eventually circled the perimeter. The next impressive formation was the five Olympic rings, then five crosses symbolising the main stars of the Southern Cross constellation — a national symbol the viewer was exposed to on a number of occasions during the evening's entertainment.

The Welcome sequence included impressive displays of riding in formation by horses and riders, a stirring fanfare, the national anthem, concluding when the last horseman left the stadium. The sequence ran for 11 minutes and 35 seconds. It was the harsh landscape and the rural clothing worn by the riders, and subsequently the musicians, that were the key Australian signifiers which stood out in the sequence. The riders were clothed in the traditional wet-weather gear of the bush rider — Driza-Bone coat, Akubra hat, RM Williams boots and moleskin trousers. The main colour shown in this opening segment was brown — the horses, the Driza-Bones and the floor surface of the stadium.

The world was then greeted with a popular colloquial Australian welcome when a huge banner was unfurled from on high. The banner contained the welcoming Aussie four letter word 'G'day' displayed in the child-like writing style that Australian artist Ken Done is famous for. At the Opening Ceremony, the 'G'day' message was written within the stylised arch of one of Australia's most recognised landmarks, the Sydney Harbour Bridge.

Deep Sea Dreaming

The transition between the opening sequence and the next is marked by signage, sound effects and stadium lighting which transformed the surface floor of the arena from the brown tones of the outback to the golden sands of Australia's coastal beaches. The sound effects heard at the beginning of the sequence were a flock of seagulls.

The Deep Sea Dreaming segment ran for eight minutes and could possibly be compared in style to Lewis Carroll's classic text *Alice in Wonderland.* The section saw 13 year-old Nikki Webster, playing the part of the 'Hero-Girl', skip into the middle of the stadium, spread out a huge beach towel, and dream about Australia's colourful seaside imagery. To highlight her vulnerability and innocence, she wore a pink sundress, with matching bag, shoes and bow in her curly blonde hair.

Stadium Australia was transformed into a three-dimensional giant fishbowl featuring oversized jellyfish, seahorses, angelfish, sea cucumbers, moray eels and other sea creatures. Such sights were presented as being reasonably familiar for the many Australians who live near the country's 36,735 kilometres of coastline, or for any tourist who has explored the Great Barrier Reef or has stepped foot on Australia's beaches including the most famous — Sydney's Bondi Beach.

Awakening

The Awakening sequence was particularly important in setting the tone of respect and reconciliation for the rest of the evening's performance. This tone continued strongly throughout the 16 days of the Olympic Games. Early in the Awakening sequence, which ran for 11 minutes and 45 seconds, Garry Wilkinson crossed to fellow commentator Ernie Dingo who introduced himself and the segment to viewers with the following words:

> G'day mob. 'Ow are ya? There's over 40,000 years of culture with 600 indigenous nations. Over 200 Aboriginal groups representing over 250,000 indigenous Australians. This is an awakening! Djakapurra, the Songman, calls the visitors to listen to the sounds of the earth — to meet an ancient past and awaken the spirits within. The young Australian girl is now a part of the land's ancient culture — hers too to share. First of all to understand the origins of where it all came from. (Seven Network, 2000)

With the Awakening segment, Stadium Australia was symbolically cleansed with the burning of eucalyptus leaves. Some may have even wondered whether white Australia's black history could be just as easily cleansed in the nation's collective consciousness. It certainly seemed that the organisers of the Opening Ceremony at least were trying to convey a message along those lines. The main colours worn by the dancers in this segment were red and yellow — which along with black — make up the colours of the Aboriginal flag.

The main formation made by the dancers was an inner and outer circle and parallel lines leading to them. Fertility and continuation of life were the messages being conveyed. The same fertility story had been communicated on cave walls for thousands of years. The emphasis is on enclosed circles representing the strong kinship of Aboriginal culture. The significant smoking ceremony took place within the circle to keep the positive spirits enclosed before later being released and shared.

While the young Nikki Webster symbolised Australia's future, Aboriginal songman and elder Djakapurra Munyarryun represented Australia's proud and ancient indigenous past. The older and wiser songman led the 'hero girl' through her fascinating journey of discovery.

In the Awakening segment the ancient spirits were ceremoniously called upon to cleanse the stadium and ensure it was ready for the various sporting events which were to take place over the forthcoming fortnight. While Ken Done's 'G'day' banner was quickly unfurled from on high in the Welcome sequence, the much larger banner of the Wandjina spirit, that comes from the Kimberley region of Western Australia, slowly rose from the surface of the stadium. The well-known 'Wandjina Spirit' painting by Charlie Numblar has come to be regarded as one of the symbols of hope for reconciliation between black and white Australia. Both banners were met with enthusiastic applause from the stadium audience. The Wandjina banner is the traditional welcome and possibly the alternative for 'G'day'. Old and new Australia are portrayed in vastly different ways but convey a similar message.

Fire

The Wandjina Spirit banner marked the end of the Awakening segment and the beginning of the Fire sequence. In the Opening Ceremony fire and flame took on greater signification than the singular role that might normally be anticipated — the crucial lighting of the cauldron. The Fire sequence, of three minutes duration, was the briefest of the seven. The natural elements of earth, wind, fire and water all had a place within the Opening Ceremony and at times more than one of the elements intersected with another.

While taking on circus-like characteristics with fire-breathing performers, the Fire segment served to reinforce the cleansing and renewal theme of the Awakening sequence. It may have also reminded Australians of the harsh environment in which they live as many Australian homes are exposed to the risk of bushfire each Summer. Australian bushfires regularly generate significant interest from international news media as a result of their size and severity. The news stories serve to reinforce the perception that Australia is a land of climatic contrasts and extreme weather conditions — a land of drought and flooding rains.

Nature

The fires then made way for the blossoming of Australia's colourful flora — spectacular wildflowers after the rains have further cleansed the earth. The sound of a kookaburra was heard in a similar way to which the seagulls marked the bird sound at the beginning of the Deep Sea Dreaming sequence. The kookaburra heralds the coming of rain in the Australian bush.

The Nature segment was the most colourful and majestic of all the sequences and ran for just over nine minutes. It featured abundant Australian flora including Australia's official floral emblem the Golden Wattle, along with the floral emblems of New South Wales, South Australia and Victoria — the Waratah, Sturt's Desert Pea and the Common Heath respectively. Once the earth had regenerated after the bushfires — an essential requirement for the rebirth — the wildlife could return. Selected Australian fauna were then displayed in the form of seven large paintings by Aboriginal artist Jeffrey Samuels.

To ensure continuity of the story, Nikki Webster and Djakapurra Munyarryun are woven back into the production. A colourful tapestry of flowers illuminates Stadium Australia. Djakapurra surveys the wonders before him but the beauty of the scene slowly fades when Captain Cook arrives and the 'Tin Symphony' segment begins.

Tin Symphony

With the exception of the Parade of Athletes, the Tin Symphony sequence was the longest, being of 13 minutes and 30 seconds duration. It commenced with Captain Cook who was depicted as a white invader with strange inventions and a preponderance to collect and classify.

Cook and his crew arrived on a stylised Endeavour ship and the not so subtle message was that they had come to change the natural order of things in this Great Southern Land. Held captive in a cage at the rear of the strange contraption was a white rabbit. The rabbit appeared to emphasise that the British had no idea how they would live in the harsh Australian environment. It was obvious that it would not take long to destroy the ancient natural balance that indigenous Australians had long nurtured, respected and protected. The white rabbit may have also served as a reminder of the *Alice in Wonderland* text, as outlined earlier. The break in the Ceremony between old and new Australia was incredibly abrupt. It was represented by a loud fireworks explosion released by Cook and immediately followed by a multitude of Ned Kelly dancers who entered the stadium with guns blazing.

The Tin Symphony sequence included the largest number of Australian icons and therefore enabled the local audience, particularly those brought up in the bush, to remember treasured rustic relics such as corrugated iron, windmills, shearing sheds and rainwater tanks. In this sequence, however, Ric Birch couldn't resist a few quirky Australian images for the rest of the world to ponder, including Victa lawnmowers (an iconic Australian brand), corrugated iron outback dunnies (toilets), dancing Ned Kellys and strange jumping cardboard boxes — which were 'meant' to symbolise sheep.

Windmills were also included in the Tin Symphony segment as both objects in their own right and as the main backbone of the giant Kelly horse (as it was referred to by the Opening Ceremony organisers) which symbolised the arrival of new technology. Windmills started to become a familiar image on the Australian horizon after artesian water basins were discovered in the 1870s. The unique Australian game of two-up was also included in the Tin Symphony sequence. The television viewer witnessed a group of men playing the game while the women watched, leaning against a corrugated iron shack. The cry 'Come in Spinner' continues to occasionally be heard at Australian casinos to this day.

Arrivals

The penultimate Arrival sequence, which ran for 11 minutes and 20 seconds, took on the atmosphere of a frenzied Mardi Gras of diasporic dimensions. Immigrants from Africa, the Americas, Oceania, Europe and Asia were represented in the five colours of the Olympic rings. The interlocked Olympic rings of blue, yellow, black, green and red (particularly when set against a white background as they are in the Olympic flag) are an extremely powerful signifier of unity as the combined colours incorporate flags from all nations. The Olympic rings are also considered to be the most recognised of all logos in the world.

The crowd was encouraged to wildly wave and flash their torches and glowing wrist bands to the hypnotic beat. Audience participation was a central aspect of the segment and images of individual spectators were shown on the big screen and at home. The crowd continued flashing their torches for Nikki Webster's emotional rendition of the all-encompassing song *Under Southern Skies*. The inclusive nature of the segment and the song was also emphasised by having a representative from each of the five Olympic regional groups behind her, and moreover the signing of the words by all performers for the benefit of the hearing impaired. When all the 2,500 performers who took part in the Arrivals segment had entered the centre of the stadium, they carefully combined to form the Australian landmass.

The other key formation featured in this sequence was that of the Southern Cross. While the Southern Cross constellation is featured on the flags of a number of countries in the Southern hemisphere such as New Zealand, Papua New Guinea and Western Samoa, it has been adopted by a range of organisations in Australia for more than 150 years. As the audience shone their torches, the Southern Cross sparkled in the middle of the arena — a symbolic representation of the night sky above the stadium.

Eternity

The final sequence, Eternity, was a tribute to the Australian working class — particularly those that physically built the nation's key landmarks, monuments and infrastructure, with 1,000 tap dancers representing the energy, confidence and enthusiasm of a young country. The segment began with a lone tap dancer and ran for almost 13 minutes. A bridge was built to symbolically connect old Australia to the new.

Appropriately Djakapurra and Nikki came together on the bridge which was lit up by the word 'Eternity'. Djakapurra then walked Nikki around the arena where all the performers from previous segments had now joined the tap dancers. We know that the story had come to an end, and that the telling of the story is indeed over, when the two stars leave the main stadium as all of the other performers had done before them — through one of the many stadium exits. Australia's story has been told, and the viewer was left to ponder the significance of what they had witnessed.

The formalities: band, athletes, speeches, flag, oath and flame

Following the creative sequences which told the story of old and new Australia, the world's largest marching band emerged. The viewer was told the Sydney 2000 Olympic Band was comprised of 'musicians of the world' and was the largest marching band to ever perform. The band members wore red, white and blue Driza-Bones, and also wore the familiar Akubra hat. While the band were taking their places and warming up, some members of the crowd burst into an impromptu "Aussie, Aussie Aussie", to which the reply is inevitably "Oi, Oi, Oi". A number of tunes and formations took place but the loudest cheer from the crowd came when the Sydney 2000 logo was formed to the tune of *Waltzing Matilda*.

The Parade of Athletes, the longest section of the evening, then followed. The host team Australia, by virtue of Olympic tradition, was the last to enter the arena. The Australian athletes in their uniforms in the colours of ochre, wattle blossom and eucalyptus leaves were led by basketball player Andrew Gaze. The music heard while the Australian athletes entered the stadium included the Australian tunes *Click Go the Shears*, *I Am Australian* and, once again, *Waltzing Matilda*.

Australian singers John Farnham and Olivia Newton-John sang the uplifting *Dare to Dream* while making their way through the pathway dividing two groups of the world's athletes gathered in the centre of the arena. The all-important speeches then took place and International Olympic Committee President Juan Antonio Samaranch welcomed the world with the patriotic words, "G'day Sydney. G'day Australia. Yes, the Olympic Games are back down under!" (Seven Network, 2000). In the final words of his speech and in keeping with the respectful theme of the evening, Samaranch paid a special tribute to Australia's Aboriginal and Torres Strait Islander people.

After the speeches came the Flag Ceremony which commenced with an enormous piece of white material covering the crowd at the southern end of the stadium. Australian singer Vanessa Amarossi reminded the athletes of their immortal place in history when she sang *Heroes Live Forever*. The reading of the oath on behalf of both athletes and officials took place, followed by the climax of the evening, the lighting of the Olympic flame.

The Opening Ceremony was capped-off with the image to be emblazoned on the front pages of the newspapers the next morning — Cathy Freeman standing under the Olympic cauldron against a backdrop of nature's contrasting elements — fire and water. After being handed the flame, Freeman held the torch aloft then proceeded to jog up the flights of stairs towards a large water feature. With great spiritual significance Freeman carefully walked across the water, again held up the flame, then leaned down to light the ring of fire. The lone athlete was surrounded by a circular blaze which roared above her, the outline of the cauldron was revealed and water simultaneously cascaded down. Freeman held her torch aloft while remaining in the centre of the circle. She then stepped out from the surrounding water to face the sheer might of the fiery cauldron.

The Channel Seven commentators couldn't hold back their enthusiasm at the choice of Cathy Freeman to light the flame. Commentator Sandy Roberts stated, "It must rank as the greatest single event in the modern history of Australia" (Seven Network, 2000). Bruce McAvaney responded, "What an inspired choice! Cathy Freeman — such a powerful statement" (Seven Network, 2000). Australian Olympic Committee President John Coates later explained to the media, "It is a very major statement that an indigenous Australian can light the flame at the Millennium Games" (Donnan, 2000). Some might argue that Sydney Olympic organisers were also wise to choose Freeman and promote the highly considerable indigenous themes throughout the Opening Ceremony. In 1988, thousands of indigenous people had protested against Australia's celebration of 200 years of white settlement with the slogans 'White Australia has a Black History' and '40,000 Years don't make a Bicentenary'.

The telling of Australia's story concludes

Commentator Bruce McAvaney was permitted the final words of the Channel Seven telecast. He summed up the night with the following:

> Well, we said at the beginning of the night that on this night all Australia was one. Well, perhaps for the last few hours, the whole world was one. And for a few minutes one person was

centre stage of the whole world. Cathy Freeman — an island in fire. What a powerful image! What an Australian image! Who will ever forget it? And how will Australia sleep tonight? Now we turn the page to 16 days of competition. The Olympic Games are a playing field for every emotion possible. Every athlete will have a story and who knows who will create the biggest headline? Tonight, it's Australia! (Seven Network, 2000).

The Opening Ceremony included much attention to detail such as the Globite school cases placed on the 110,000 seats in Stadium Australia. The cases contained a torch, flashing wristband, official programme, stickers, pin and other souvenirs to remember the event. The stadium floor was particularly impressive — designed to resemble the Australian outback viewed from above.

Generally, most Australians were relieved that the Ceremony was free of the clichés we had become so accustomed to seeing in television advertising and tourism brochures. Many Australians were apprehensive because Ric Birch had let them down before, with a giant Matilda kangaroo at the 1982 Commonwealth Games in Brisbane, and the inflatable kangaroos on bikes at the Atlanta Games in 1996. To the relief of the nation, Birch managed to impress the world with what was by and large a sophisticated display of national identity that had been six years in the making.

While the Driza-Bones and Akubras were out in force, the highly stereotyped images of Australia's most famous fauna (kangaroos and koalas) were virtually non-existent. Even Sydney Olympic mascots Syd, Millie and Olly became nocturnal creatures that night. We were to soon discover however that the clichés and overt stereotypes would be saved for the Closing Ceremony. Ric Birch even made sure that the infamous blow-up kangaroo on bicycle made an appearance, and he chose to ride the bike!

The Australian signifiers that were included in the Opening Ceremony were not selected from a narrow stereotypical repertoire but covered a wide variety of representations of Australia, Australians and Australianness. The signifiers could be generally classified under the headings — flags, colours, landscape, landmarks, artefacts, pre-1788 references, post-1788 references, clothes, plants, animals, words, music and songs.

But while Birch was portrayed as something of an antagonist, Australians may have been their own worst enemy. Whether we are prepared to admit it or not, we are a nation of knockers who are quick to criticise — even before an event. Australians are generally quick to cut down tall poppies — the elite. Even in this new millennium we are a highly self-conscious nation preoccupied with what the rest of the world thinks of us. And in the usual navel-gazing tradition, the Australian media spent significant air time and print space reporting on what the rest of the world made of our Opening Ceremony — particularly the Aussie oddities such as the Victa lawnmowers and sheep in cardboard boxes.

But we need not have worried — Ric Birch showed the diversity of Australia in all its glory for the Sydney Olympic Games Opening Ceremony. He retold Australia's story with a new and fresh perspective to the general relief and gratification of Australian audiences, and to the fascination and delight of international audiences. Australia's story had been told, a story of old and new Australia, and it was gripping enough to hold the attention 3.5 billion viewers on 15 September, 2000. Ric Birch appeared to have successfully orchestrated a large-scale celebration of the Australian nation without the cultural cringe.

References

Berelson, B. (1952) *Content analysis in communication research*. New York: Hafner Press.

Bingham-Hall, P. (ed) (2000) *Celebrating Sydney 2000: 100 Legacies*. Balmain, NSW: Pesaro Publishing.

Cameron, D. (2000) 'A message or two before thankyou, and goodnight', *The Sydney Morning Herald*, Sydney, 1 October, <http://www.olympics.smh.com.au/new/2000/10/01/ffxlesvtrdc.html>

Culler, J. (1995) 'The consumption of tourism', in J. Urry (ed) *Consuming places*. London: Routledge.

Donnan, S. (2000) 'Aboriginal star rises above Aussie history', *Christian Science Monitor*, 19 September, <http://www.csmonitor/oly2000/stories/0919donnan.html>

Fiske, J. (1990) *Introduction to communication studies*. London: Routledge.

Larson, J. F. and Park, H. S. (1993) *Global television and the politics of the Seoul Olympics*. Boulder, Colorado: Westview Press.

Leiss, W., Kline, S. and Jhally S. (1990) *Social communication in advertising: Persons, products, and images of well-being (Second Edition)*. Scarborough, Ontario: Nelson.

Lenskyj, H. J. (2002) *The best Olympics ever? Social impacts of Sydney 2000*. Albany: State University of New York Press.

News Limited and Harper Collins Publishers (2000a) *Unbeatable Sydney: The complete Olympic record*. Pymble: NSW.

News Limited and Harper Collins Publishers (2000b) *2000 Australian Olympic Team Handbook and Media Guide*. Pymble: NSW.

Seven Network (2000) *Sydney 2000 Opening Ceremony*, 15 September.

Veal, A. J. and Lynch, R. (2001) *Australian leisure (Second Edition)*. Frenchs Forest, NSW: Longman.

Warneke, R. (2000) 'Games win gold', *The Age* (Green Guide supplement), Melbourne, 28 September, p. 6.

Webb, T. (2001) *The collaborative games: The story behind the spectacle*. Annandale, NSW: Pluto Press Australia.

Leisure Studies Association

LSA Publications

LSA

An extensive list of publications on a wide range of leisure studies topics, produced by the Leisure Studies Association since the late 1970s, is available from LSA Publications.

Some of the more recently published volumes are detailed on the following pages, and full information may be obtained on newer and forthcoming LSA volumes from:

LSA Publications, c/o M. McFee
email: mcfee@solutions-inc.co.uk
The Chelsea School, University of Brighton
Eastbourne BN20 7SP (UK)

Among other benefits, members of the Leisure Studies Association may purchase LSA Publications at preferential rates. Please contact LSA at the above address for information regarding membership of the Association, LSA Conferences, and LSA Newsletters.

ONLINE

Complete information about LSA Publications:

www.leisure-studies-association.info/LSAWEB/Publications.html

EVALUATING SPORT AND ACTIVE LEISURE FOR YOUNG PEOPLE

**LSA Publication No. 88.   ISBN: 0 906337 99 2 [2005] pp. 236+xviii
eds. Kevyn Hylton, Anne Flintoff and Jonathan Long**

Contents

LSA Publication No. 88. (cont.)

YOUTH SPORT AND ACTIVE LEISURE: THEORY, POLICY AND PARTICIPATION

**LSA Publication No. 87.   ISBN: 0 906337 98 4 [2005] pp. 185 + xii
eds. Anne Flintoff, Jonathan Long and Kevyn Hylton**

Contents

SPORT AND ACTIVE LEISURE YOUTH CULTURES

**LSA PUBLICATIONS NO. 86. ISBN: 0 906337 97 6 [2005] pp. 238 + xxii
eds. Jayne Caudwell and Peter Bramham**

Contents

LEISURE, SPACE AND VISUAL CULTURE: PRACTICES AND MEANINGS

LSA Publication No. 84. ISBN: 0 906337 95 X [2004] pp. 292+xxii
eds. Cara Aitchison and Helen Pussard

Contents

LEISURE, MEDIA AND VISUAL CULTURE: REPRESENTATIONS AND CONTESTATIONS

**LSA Publication No. 83. ISBN: 0 906337 94 1 [2004] pp. 282
eds. Eileen Kennedy and Andrew Thornton**

Contents

SPORT, LEISURE AND SOCIAL INCLUSION

**LSA Publication No. 82. ISBN: 0 906337 933 [2003] pp. 296
ed. Adrian Ibbetseon, Beccy Watson and Maggie Ferguson**

Contents

ACCESS AND INCLUSION IN LEISURE AND TOURISM

**LSA Publication No. 81. ISBN: 0 906337 92 5 [2003] pp. 288
eds. Bob Snape, Edwin Thwaites, Christine Williams**

Contents

VOLUNTEERS IN SPORT

**LSA Publication No. 80. ISBN: 0 906337 91 7 [2003] pp. 107
ed. Geoff Nichols**

Contents

LEISURE CULTURES: INVESTIGATIONS IN SPORT, MEDIA AND TECHNOLOGY

LSA Publication No. 79. ISBN: 0 906337 90 9 [2003] pp. 221 + xii
eds. Scott Fleming and Ian Jones

Contents

PARTNERSHIPS IN LEISURE: SPORT, TOURISM AND MANAGEMENT

LSA Publication No. 78. ISBN: 0 906337 89 5 [2002] pp. 245 + iv
eds. Graham Berridge and Graham McFee

Contents

LEISURE STUDIES:
TRENDS IN THEORY AND RESEARCH

**LSA Publication No. 77. ISBN: 0 906337 88 7 [2001] pp. 198 + iv
eds. Stan Parker and Lesley Lawrence**

Contents

SPORT TOURISM: PRINCIPLES AND PRACTICE

**LSA Publication No. 76. ISBN: 0 906337 87 9 [2001] pp. 174 + xii
eds. Sean Gammin and Joseph Kurtzman**

Contents

VOLUNTEERING IN LEISURE: MARGINAL OR INCLUSIVE?

LSA Publication No. 75. ISBN: 0 906337 86 0 [2001] pp. 158+xi eds. Margaret Graham and Malcolm Foley

Contents

LEISURE CULTURES, CONSUMPTION AND COMMODIFICATION

**LSA Publication No. 74. ISBN: 0 906337 85 2 [2001] pp. 158+xi
ed. John Horne**

Contents

LEISURE AND SOCIAL INCLUSION: NEW CHALLENGES FOR POLICY AND PROVISION

LSA Publication No. 73. ISBN: 0 906337 84 4 [2001] pp. 204
eds. Gayle McPherson and Malcolm Reid

Contents

JUST LEISURE:
EQUITY, SOCIAL EXCLUSION AND IDENTITY

LSA Publication No 72. ISBN: 0 906337 83 6 [2000] pp. 195+xiv
Edited by Celia Brackenridge, David Howe and Fiona Jordan

Contents

JUST LEISURE: POLICY, ETHICS & PROFESSIONALISM

LSA Publication No 71. ISBN: 0 906337 81 X [2000] pp. 257+xiv
Edited by Celia Brackenridge, David Howe and Fiona Jordan

Contents

WOMEN'S LEISURE EXPERIENCES: AGES, STAGES AND ROLES

LSA Publication No. 70. ISBN 0 906337 80 1 [2001]
Edited by Sharon Clough and Judy White

Contents

MASCULINITIES: LEISURE CULTURES, IDENTITIES AND CONSUMPTION

LSA Publication No. 69. ISBN: 0 906337 77 1 [2000] pp. 163

Edited by John Horne and Scott Fleming

Contents

GENDER ISSUES IN WORK AND LEISURE

LSA Publication No. 68.ISBN 0 906337 78 X
Edited by Jenny Anderson and Lesley Lawrence [pp. 173]

Contents

SPORT, LEISURE IDENTITIES AND GENDERED SPACES

LSA Publication No. 67. ISBN: 0 906337 79 8 [1999] pp. 196
Edited by Sheila Scraton and Becky Watson

Contents

HER OUTDOORS: RISK, CHALLENGE AND ADVENTURE IN GENDERED OPEN SPACES

LSA Publication No. 66 [1999] ISBN: 0 906337 76 3; pp. 131
Edited by Barbara Humberstone

Contents

POLICY AND PUBLICS

LSA Publication No. 65. ISBN: 0 906337 75 5 [1999] pp. 167
Edited by Peter Bramham and Wilf Murphy

Contents

CONSUMPTION AND PARTICIPATION: LEISURE, CULTURE AND COMMERCE

LSA Publication No. 64. ISBN: 0 906337 74 7 [2000]
Edited by Garry Whannel

Contents

GENDER, SPACE AND IDENTITY: LEISURE, CULTURE AND COMMERCE

LSA Publication No. 63. ISBN: 0 906337 73 9 [1998] pp. 191
Edited by Cara Aitchison and Fiona Jordan

Contents

THE PRODUCTION AND CONSUMPTION OF SPORT CULTURES: LEISURE, CULTURE AND COMMERCE

LSA Publication No. 62. ISBN: 0 906337 72 0 [1998] pp. 178
Edited by Udo Merkel, Gill Lines, Ian McDonald

Contents

TOURISM AND VISITOR ATTRACTIONS: LEISURE, CULTURE AND COMMERCE

LSA Publication No 61. ISBN: 0 906337 71 2 [1998] pp. 211
Edited by Neil Ravenscroft, Deborah Philips and Marion Bennett

Contents

LEISURE PLANNING IN TRANSITORY SOCIETIES

LSA Publication No. 58. ISBN: 0 906337 70 4
Edited by Mike Collins; pp 218

Contents

LEISURE, TIME AND SPACE: MEANINGS AND VALUES IN PEOPLE'S LIVES

LSA Publication No. 57. ISBN: 0 906337 68 2 [1998] pp. 198 + IV
Edited by Sheila Scraton

Contents

LEISURE, TOURISM AND ENVIRONMENT (I) SUSTAINABILITY AND ENVIRONMENTAL POLICIES

LSA Publication No. 50 Part I; ISBN 0 906337 64 X
Edited by Malcolm Foley, David McGillivray and Gayle McPherson (1999);

Contents

LEISURE, TOURISM AND ENVIRONMENT (II) PARTICIPATION, PERCEPTIONS AND PREFERENCES

LSA Publication No. 50 (Part II) ISBN: 0 906337 69 0; pp. 177+xii
Edited by Malcolm Foley, Matt Frew and Gayle McPherson

Contents

LEISURE: MODERNITY, POSTMODERNITY AND LIFESTYLES

LSA Publications No. 48 (LEISURE IN DIFFERENT WORLDS Volume I)
Edited by Ian Henry (1994); ISBN: 0 906337   52 6, pp. 375+

Contents

LSA Publications No. 48 (cont.)